JOHN FRANCOME

Twice Lucky

Illustrated by
GRAHAM THOMPSON

HEADLINE

First published in 1988 by Pelham Books

First published in paperback in 1989
by HEADLINE BOOK PUBLISHING PLC

Editor Michael Leitch
Designed by Cooper Wilson
Typeset by Goodfellow & Egan

ISBN 0 7472 3382 9

Printed and bound in Finland
by Werner Söderström Oy

HEADLINE BOOK PUBLISHING PLC
Headline House
79 Great Titchfield Street
London W1P 7FN

CONTENTS

FOREWORD

At my first interview with Fred Winter I was shown into his office with my dad. He looked me over quietly while I told him how much riding I had done up till then. When I had finished, he nodded. 'You're a big lad,' he said. 'We'd better put you on the scales.'

I got on these bathroom scales so he could weigh me. I came in at about 10 stone 4 lb. 'Hmm,' he said. 'That is quite heavy for a lad your age. Tell me, what's the lightest you have ever been?'

I said, 'Seven pounds four ounces.'

He took me on. It must have been out of curiosity. Even now, three years since I packed up riding, I don't think I have changed that much. I am equally sure that I am not the only jockey or ex-jockey with this outlook.

You don't have to be mad to take up horse-riding, but once you start jump-racing you find you are in a game that is too dangerous for life to be taken too seriously. No matter who you are, the champion jockey or a novice at the bottom of the ladder, you are fair game for the practical jokers in the weighing room and all the other places they lurk, and that is how it should be.

Some people plan their working lives with their eyes mainly on what they will be able to do when they retire. Jockeys don't think that way. They learn that the present is easier to deal with if you don't expect a particularly long future. 'You don't come back,' they say, 'so you might as well enjoy it now.'

This book is a kind of small monument to the jump-racer's philosophy of short futures and merry presents. You might as well enjoy it, and I hope you do.

WHAT THE TRAINER SAID TO THE JOCKEY

Racing Instructions – And What They Really Mean

It's not that trainers exactly set out to mislead jockeys. Their problem in this less-than-perfect world is that one or two things haven't been done which ought to have been done, and very few of their horses are as good as they would like them to be – or as good as they thought they were when they bought them.

This means that the truth must be embroidered here and there so that the trainer can present an acceptable face to the people he does business with. Jockeys understand this, and make their own adjustments.

For example, the trainer meets the jockey in the paddock and says, 'I haven't schooled him for a while. When you take him down, make sure you show him the first fence so he gets the feel of it.' To the jockey this is a clear admission that the horse hasn't jumped a fence in its life.

In similar fashion, if the trainer says, 'He's a bit keen so just watch him,' the jockey knows the horse will try and run off with him going to the start. At least this is more reassuring than when the trainer says, 'He's *very* keen,' which means he will run off with him before the start and during the race as well.

You get the occasional trainer who goes in for real obscurity, putting things in such a way that the jockey doesn't know whether he is joking or whether the horse really is a disaster. 'Does it jump well?' I asked a trainer on the 'phone one day after he'd asked me to ride his horse. 'Well, it did this morning,' he replied, 'when I shook a can of stones behind it.' I decided that his real meaning was, 'I don't know. But you'll find out soon enough if you ride it.'

Not all the trainer's words are addressed to jockeys. Sometimes it's the owner who has to be kept in the dark. 'Oh,' the trainer might say, 'he's a nice horse but he's a bit slow.' This means that the horse will never do anything unless it's over three miles in the mud.

If the horse is 'very slow' this, curiously enough, means exactly what it sounds like; also that the horse will never, ever, win a race. Guaranteed. And will probably end up as a hunter.

It is also, by the way, very much in the jockey's interests to be nice to owners. To go further, it is occupational suicide to tell an owner that his horse is a pile of crap. Owners are attached to their horses by invisible but immensely strong ties of sentiment and money, and they do not want to hear anything unpleasant said about any of their animals. Offend against this unwritten law, and the jockey will not ride for that owner again.

For the benefit of jockeys who find it hard to suppress their true feelings after they have been thrown or finished badly on a useless horse, here are some samples of the right thing to say to an owner:

'Well, he's a nice horse, but perhaps he wants a bit further.'

Also, 'Yes, he gave me a nice ride and he should definitely win a race.' (Thinks: 'Even if he is inside a greyhound at the time.')

Even, 'Yes, I can see why you like him. He's got nice ears, hasn't he?'

When I was riding, I never really minded all this double-talk. In fact I quite enjoyed most of it, and underneath it all nearly everyone involved realizes that, in a sport as uncertain as racing, people are bound to come out with a lot of over-optimistic rubbish. It doesn't do any harm, and it helps to keep the social wheels turning if everyone tries to be pleasant to each other.

Now and again a jockey meets an apparently meticulous trainer who goes way over the top with a whole string of detailed racing instructions. 'When you leave the paddock, take it down in front. Keep it on its own until the start, then get it into sixth or seventh. Move it up to fifth by the time you jump the third. Go round the inside and make sure you don't get behind Loppylegs because it's a bad jumper. Don't go to the front too quickly. Keep it in third until . . .'

The longer he goes on, the more certain the jockey can be that he is living in a fantasy world and everything he says can be taken with a bigger and bigger pinch of salt. What this type of trainer tends to overlook are the 101 other things that happen in a race, the totally unexpected tricks and accidents pulled by the other horses and jockeys which make racing what it is – a trial in which quick-wittedness is just as important as the speed, strength and stamina of the horse. A jockey will win very few races if he doesn't allow himself the room to think things out for himself and ride the race according to how it unfolds during the four or five minutes it takes to run it.

Another thing the jockey has to bear in mind is that the trainer may be giving him completely wrong instructions because he doesn't want the horse to win. When I was a kid I remember a trainer saying, 'Hold it up. Hold it up and come with a late run at the end.'

I had never ridden this horse before, so I tried to do what the trainer had said but all the horse wanted to do was keep galloping. Because I was able to restrain it at least some of the way, we got nowhere. The trainer didn't seem all that upset, and next time I rode the horse he said, 'Don't hold it up. Make the running on it.' Again I followed instructions and it bolted home.

Of course, this time they had their money on it.

One area where the jockey can expect no co-operation at all is if the horse has something wrong with it. It is against everything that trainers stand for to admit that a horse has broken down anywhere except on the racecourse. A trainer never wants to confess to anybody that a horse went lame at home. The owner would think he wasn't looking after it properly, and the jockey certainly wouldn't want to ride it.

The trainer avoids the stigma of incompetence by not saying anything. The jockey gets on the horse, jumps two hurdles on it and then its leg suddenly gives way so the jockey pulls it up. 'Oh, dear me,' says the trainer to the owner, 'look at that. It's broken down. That's bad luck. We've had nothing wrong with it in training.' Whereas in reality it's had a bad leg for several days and has been stood in the stable all that time doing nothing.

Unless the jockey rides out at the stable in question, he has little or no chance of finding out that there is something wrong with the horse. Perhaps the worst thing of all is to get to the racecourse and be sitting in the weighing room when another jockey says, 'Go on, why are you riding that?'

'What do you mean?' you say. 'That's a good ride.'

'No, no. I watched it schooling the other morning and it fell twice.'

Thanks for nothing, you think, and have to get on the horse and ride it while all the time you are waiting for it to bury you.

Even when things are at their bleakest, a jockey has to try and be positive. Be nice to the trainer and the owner, those are first principles if he wants to go on getting rides. Unlike the jockey who stormed in off the course one day and went straight up to the owner.

'That horse,' he shouted. 'That horse isn't a shithouse. It's a whole row of them.'

THE RACING DIARY

Around The Racecourses Of England – Some Of The Things A Jockey Looks Forward To Each Week

When a jockey looks at his racing diary for the coming week, he thinks of many things. What he most wants at the end of the week is a big meeting when he will be riding good horses in big races with attractive prize money. Cheltenham, Ascot – those are the events he most looks forward to. They offer the prospect of excitement and atmosphere on a scale he will not expect to find on the other three or four days.

Warwick on Tuesday, the very image of mundane racing, is not going to set him alight, of that he can be sure. The fields will be large and for the most part undistinguished, the track big and made for galloping with the target golf course in the middle, fences coming quickly in the back straight, a lot of pressure for space early on – the kind of track that favours a good jumper that knows what it's doing. But not a lot of good jumpers go to Warwick, do they.

Perhaps that is a little hard on Warwick. It is not the worst course in England, but it happens to be one where I didn't do very well. Racing is personal that way. It is personal to jockeys in ways that other people would not recognize. Out of a range of average courses, the jockey likes the ones with the softer fences – the ones where his horse can make a bad mistake and get away with it. At Ascot, when a horse makes a bad mistake it will invariably fall, as it will at Cheltenham, Newbury, Haydock and Wetherby. It's probably not good for the horse to think it can jump badly and get away with it, but just for the moment I am seeing it from the jockey's point of view.

The good news, as he looks at his racing diary, is that he is unlikely to be bored for very long, if at all. This country has racecourses of a variety and quality that are the envy of the world. There are fifty-three National Hunt courses in all, and we do not have the space to review each one, but this selective tour will show up the essential differences between quite a few of them.

We start in the West. Newton Abbot has a holiday atmosphere. They hold a lot of meetings early in the season to catch the holidaymakers who are down in Torquay and the other resorts nearby. The sight of those crowds, plus the go-kart track in the middle of the course and the railway line running along one side, produce a mood which is special to the place. The track is left-handed and very sharp, the ground hard in autumn, and there's no mistaking it for anywhere else.

Just up the road you come to Heldon, which is generally known as Devon & Exeter. This is right-handed, a big long galloping course with woods around two sides of it, situated beside the main Plymouth road. It has a very long uphill finish; almost every stride of the last mile and a quarter or so is uphill, and it is a stiff tiring track. Somebody came in there one day without his horse; he explained that he had been turning for home in the lead when a deer jumped out of the wood, ran straight into his horse and killed it. The weather had been a bit foggy, so nobody else had seen it. In the weighing room they gave him a lot of funny looks, and the general view was that he must have fallen off and got concussed.

Further north again, in Somerset, is Wincanton. Right-handed, much sharper than Devon & Exeter, it has a downhill finish. For the jockey this means that horses very seldom come from behind after the last fence has been jumped. By that stage in the race the leading horse will be galloping off down the slope and it is that much more difficult to peg him back.

Across the River Severn is Chepstow. This is a left-handed, very undulating course. You run up a steep hill going past the stands, then you run down, then up again, and the last hundred yards to the finishing post is downhill. It's a fair course, with a long straight, so no excuses for getting boxed in. The ground is either very soft or very firm; it never seems to be in-between at Chepstow.

Back along the M4, you go past the turning for Lambourn, mecca of the steeplechasing world, and a few miles down the road you come to Newbury, probably the best steeplechase track you will find anywhere. It's basically a flat track, left-handed, and there is always lots of room which makes it a fair course for everybody. The fences are stiff and take a lot of jumping. You need to have a good horse to succeed at Newbury.

Next is Sandown Park, near Esher, which produces some of the best finishes in the country. It is a right-handed course with a very fast back straight where the ground usually stays firm and the horses gallop quickly over it. Along the far side are three critical jumps known as the Railway Fences because the trains to London pass alongside them. These fences come together very quickly, quicker than any other fences in England. The jumping of those is very often what makes the difference between victory and defeat. Then there is a stiff uphill finish which produces some fantastic final stages. A horse may be well out in front, then suddenly it tires halfway up the hill and something comes from behind and beats it. The best finish I have ever seen in a horse race was the Whitbread Gold Cup a couple of years ago. Five horses crossed the line with only a length covering all five of them. The winner was the Queen Mother's horse, Special Cargo, ridden by Kevin Mooney and trained by Fulke Walwyn.

Virtually next-door to Sandown, at Sunbury, is Kempton Park. This course gets the biggest crowd of all on Boxing Day because that is when they run the King George VI Chase. On other days, though, especially in the midweek races, there is very little atmosphere. It's a flat, right-handed course with a great big reservoir next to the track. I used to enjoy racing there, but that was mainly because I had a lot of winners. Maybe it's the suburban setting, but for some reason Kempton doesn't have the impact it ought to except on the very big occasions.

Plumpton, in East Sussex, has two main characteristics. It is a great place to go to for a day out – and a horrible place to ride round. At the start of the two-mile events you run down a very steep hill and, if your horse is having its first run over hurdles and doesn't make a good job of the first two, you are out of the race. After the hill you go round a sharp left-hand bend by the railway, then turn into the straight which is uphill. It's a very tight circuit, just a mile round. I didn't mind riding there when the going was soft, but in summer, when the ground was firm, it was a nightmare going down that hill on something that wasn't jumping well, surrounded by eighteen other runners.

Fontwell, between Arundel and Chichester, is a lovely course. The 'chase course is a figure-of-eight and the hurdle course is left-handed. It's set on the side of a hill, but it's less steep than Plumpton and the fences seem to ride a lot better. It's also a very good spectator course, and that's where I always take someone who is going racing for the first time. You can watch them jump the first hurdle, then wander across and see them jump the last. It's a stiff uphill finish, with always a good crowd and plenty of atmosphere. Fontwell is a very nice little course.

Lingfield, in Surrey, is popular with the punters because it's an easy train journey down from London and a very pretty course as well. Jockeys like it because the wings of the fences are natural hedges, so if a horse runs out you don't go crashing through a lot of wood. Very often, too, the ground is so bad at that time of year (December) there are fewer runners and, when you can go round with six or seven others rather than sixteen, it's much more enjoyable, like a good day's hunting.

Now down to Folkestone, one of the coldest racecourses in England. I used to love riding at Folkestone. Fred Winter very seldom had runners there but John Jenkins always had a lot and so did many of my other trainers. One of the best things was being able to go all the way there by train and not have the hassle of driving. We used to have a bit of a laugh going across London on the Tube and then catch the punters' train to Folkestone. Just once in a while something would go wrong, like the day four of us went down there for a meeting just before Christmas.

We were already late, and then the train didn't stop at Westenhanger, by the racecourse, but went straight on to the next place. When we got out there were no taxis in sight, so I asked an old lady sitting in her car if she would drive us to the races. She wound up her window as if frightened we were going to mug her, so I ran up the road and found a guy plucking some turkeys next to his house. He had an old Morris pickup parked outside; I gave him a fiver and he took us all up to the racecourse on the back of this pickup. It was freezing cold, I can remember, and it turned out to be a waste of a fiver. Three of us were riding the three most fancied horses in the first race, and none of us could finish closer than fifth.

All the same, I like blowy old Folkestone. It's a right-handed course, the fences are nice and easy, and going down there makes a very pleasant change.

Jump to the Midlands and you come to Huntingdon, probably the most boring racecourse on earth. Right-handed, very flat, you get a lot of fast races there. It is set beside some gravel pits next to the A1; the weighing room food is dreadful; the weighing room doubles as a changing room for the football and rugby club and has outstandingly poor facilities, always cold and damp. Bad horses run there, you get bad racing and it's a bloody awful place to get to. Apart from that, there's nothing wrong with it.

Moving west, you come to Towcester, in Northamptonshire. This is another cold place, with a very stiff right-handed track. You jump three fences going downhill, then you run along the bottom and for the last mile or so it's all uphill – and a good deal stiffer than Devon & Exeter or the hill at Cheltenham. Towcester is probably the steepest hill of the lot, and it can be a killer. As for the facilities, the changing room is pretty abysmal, but the food is quite good; the two old boys in charge of the catering do a great job. It must be the only racecourse changing room in the country which has wooden seats on the toilets. I'll tell you something else: if you go in the one on the right, you have to be quick when you pull the chain, or else water rushes out over your head from the cistern. It's been like that for about ten years.

ESH PLUCKED
URKEYS

Warwick I have already dealt with. This little tour of the courses is really limited to the southern half of the country, and that is where I had most of my rides. When it's Grand National time, of course, everyone converges on Liverpool. I never enjoyed staying up there, so I used to come back home each night. The course is left-handed, as most people with a television should know by now. The fences on the National course are very good and, if you are on a good jumper, it's a thrill to ride round them. If you are on a bad jumper, it's horrible. You know you won't get far, and the race becomes a question of when you're going to fall, not if, which is a jockey's nightmare. I rode a horse up there one year which I had never seen before. I got to the paddock, saw it, and if I could have, I would have walked straight back inside and refused to have ridden it. It was very small, and when I got on it I had a feeling that its legs were tied together. In the race, it surprised me by jumping everything. In its own time, mark you, but it did jump round and finished last. When we came in, the owners thought I hadn't given it a ride, so they got somebody else to ride it next time out, at Cheltenham. It turned three somersaults going down the hill there. Some horses like to do things in their own time.

The other racing at Liverpool is on the Mildmay course, which is a very sharp track and very difficult. The ground is nearly always fast, the turns are bad and two fences are very badly sited – the fence turning for home and the ditch in the straight. The speed of the track plus the difficulty of the fences means you always get a lot of fallers.

Between Liverpool and Manchester is Haydock. It's a good, fair course, quite similar to Newbury. The fences are testing, and some have a steep drop to them which horses take a while to get used to. You get good horses there, and good racing too.

Finally, Cheltenham. At the Festival meetings there is a tremendous atmosphere, with a big contingent of Irish over for the week. Winners always get a great reception, and I've never forgotten the welcome they gave Jonjo O'Neill when he won the Gold Cup on Dawn Run. From a jockey's point of view it is less easy during the Festival to ride the race you want. I always liked to run round the inside, which at an ordinary meeting was usually possible, but in the big races it was much more difficult to do what you wanted, and really a matter of luck whether or not you got stopped on the turn at the top of the hill. I think I've fallen at every fence at Cheltenham. I broke my arm there on the second race I ever rode. They have a bunch of blokes who drive around in Land Rovers to bring the jockeys back, and I know most of them by their first name.

From that little round-up I hope you will see what a good assortment of courses we have in England – a variety of shapes, undulations and goings that change constantly throughout the season. You get everything. You start in the autumn at Newton Abbot and the ground has got cracks in it. You go through to Lingfield in December when they will be having a job to race at all; it's so wet it's almost up to their hocks. You finish up on rock-hard ground at somewhere like Ludlow or Cartmel. In between you get all sorts of things – fogged off, snowed off, frosted off, rained off, and yet at some stage in the season there will be something to suit everyone.

ESPECIALLY WHEN YOU LAUGH

The Average Apprentice Enjoys Himself So Much In His First Two Years, He Is Hooked For Life On Racing

I had been riding since the age of seven, and shortly before I started as an apprentice with Fred Winter I had been working with showjumpers. This gave me an insight into looking after horses which a lot of apprentices never got until they actually began at the stables. Some came from the East End of London and had never been near a horse in their lives.

What I quickly found out was that, although you may do things a certain way at a showjumping stable, it is very different when you are looking after racehorses. On my first morning I walked down into the yard, got my mucksack and pitchfork and went off to muck out the first horse. I had my transistor radio with me, so I put it on.

Every horse in the yard went mad. Three or four broke their head collars and one got loose onto Fred Winter's lawn, and there was chaos for several minutes before the head lad got everything calmed down enough to come over and give me my first bollocking. Not a great start.

Working with the showjumpers, I had also got into a bad habit with the tacking-up routine. Very often, if a horse had its head over the stable door, we used to put the bridle on it from the outside, then open the door and go in and finish the job. In a racing stable, you open the door first of all, go in and put a head collar on the horse, dress it over, pick its feet out and then tack it up. When the head lad saw me doing it my way, only minutes after the first bollocking, he quickly came over and gave me a second one. Things were happening so fast that morning, I nearly got sent home before I had begun.

After that we all settled down together and I began to enjoy myself. They were good days and I was staying in a good hostel, which counts for a lot. It was clean and we were well fed. The toilet facilities would not have won four roses from a hotel inspector but that was more because of overcrowding than because they didn't work. I knew I was in a good hostel because one day I went over to see some of the lads at another yard. They were living like pigs: sleeping in their wellingtons and jodhpurs in unmade beds in rooms that smelt of old socks and dustbins. We might well have gone the same way in our hostel but, fortunately, we had a couple of older lads living there who kept us up to the mark.

I worked as an apprentice for two years and then moved up a rung to be a stable lad. The rules governing apprenticeships are less formal than they used to be and you won't find many young school-leavers nowadays taking out five-year indentures, whether to become a stable lad or to take up some other kind of trade. What I most remember about being an apprentice was that you did all the dirty jobs and you did what you were told. It was like being a fag at a public school.

When the horses were fed, it was the apprentices who had to stay behind and wash out the mash barrow, clean the feed house and the tack room and make sure everything was in good order. When you finally got in for your meal, very often the older lads had already swiped the best part of it. Last thing at night you had to go down and put the rugs on the horses and shut all the top doors. Then, if a couple of the older lads decided they wanted a few bottles from the pub, it was one of the apprentices who had to go out and fetch them.

I found being at the bottom of the heap quite difficult to accept at first. Having had all those years of experience with horses, then being treated like a total beginner alongside other apprentices who *were* total beginners – that didn't really suit me but I got used to it. Nobody really likes doing all the mucky jobs, and it's only natural to look forward to a time when you can stop doing them. Everyone else goes through it, and at the end of each season a new batch of apprentices arrive and you are no longer the lowest of the low. You may even become the head apprentice, in which case you only supervise the making of the mash instead of doing all the shovelling.

ESPECIALLY WHEN YOU LAUGH

Money was what I needed most of all. I was saving up to buy a car when I went to Fred Winter's, and to earn more cash I used to clean the head lad's car and the Governor's as well, and in the evenings go babysitting. That was always a good perk,sitting in someone's house – which was always more comfortable than the hostel – and being paid for it. And getting stuck into their larder as well.

The whole point of being an apprentice – as long as you didn't grow too fast – was to make progress with your riding until one day you became a jockey. Those who couldn't ride when they came to the stable got their first instruction on the Governor's ponies. They did that in the afternoons until they could ride to a reasonable standard and then they would be allowed to ride a racehorse round the lanes for a few weeks or months, depending on how they picked it up. Then they would ride a canter, and eventually they would ride work, and if they were still good enough they would be able to go schooling, where the horses are trained over hurdles and fences.

It's a gradual process. Bit by bit the apprentice gathers the skills he needs for his ultimate profession. It is a difficult and physically exacting period, and the good apprentice is expected to work hard, keep his nose clean and bide his time. That also means not being too cocky and pretending you know more than you do.

After riding work, the horses were lined up while the trainer came past and asked each lad or apprentice how it had gone or what happened. I remember we had a lad who thought he knew a bit, and on the first morning he had ever ridden work the Governor walked down the line and stopped next to him.

'How was he?' asked the Governor, eyeing the horse which happened to be one of his particular favourites.

'He'd be better off between a couple of shafts, Governor,' came the answer.

With that simple and not very witty sentence the lad virtually committed occupational suicide. The Governor was so stunned by what he had heard, I don't think he even said anything, but as he passed quietly on to the next horse the lad was left in no doubt that he had seriously overstepped the mark.

Few trainers have them any more, but when I was an apprentice we had these old horses who were known as schoolmasters. Their main job was to lead the young horses and also to teach the apprentices how to jump. A typical schoolmaster would be a horse which had raced a lot and now was virtually retired, perhaps running once or twice a year.

For the apprentice it was a marvellous introduction because the old horse knew it all and the rider had to do nothing more than sit on it. We had a lovely old schoolmaster called Kilkoran who did everything for you, and when you had got the hang of jumping the baby hurdles with him, and then the bigger ones, you would move on to ride a horse that wasn't so competent. Up on the schooling ground they have three different-sized hurdles and three different-sized fences – the largest being the size you get on a racecourse – and every apprentice works his way through them, just as the horses do.

In the meantime the apprentice also gets to know a bit about the funny ways of horses. Like when they decide to get down on the ground and have a roll. We had a lad whose horse suddenly did this and it scared the wits out of him. Admittedly, the horse looked as if it was going to break a brand-new saddle, but this wasn't what upset the lad. He shouted for the Governor to come back quickly – convinced that the horse was dying. The Governor turned back to look, saw the horse having a nice roll on the grass and blew a fuse. The poor old lad didn't know where to look when he realized how stupid he'd been; it's all just part of the never-ending process of learning about horses.

A lot of apprentices used their free time in the afternoon, from about one o'clock until four, to have a sleep. Others played football. Then it was evening stables, and after that it was up to us. We had a pool table and a dart board in our hostel and we either played those or cards, or watched television.

Down at the pub they also had a dart board and we played a lot of matches against teams from other yards. I was a very moderate darts player and in the first match I ever played, down at the Red Lion in Lambourn, I was soon falling behind. Then one of my team put me right.

'You'll have to pull your finger out, John,' he warned me, 'because the loser has to buy the winner a drink.'

That was bad news to me. I was saving up to buy a car and only had a threepenny bit in my pocket. (This must have been a long time ago.) So I made a big recovery and just pipped him on the last dart.

Every Friday or Saturday night there was a dance in the village and, when we wanted more variety, we hired a taxi and drove into Swindon or Newbury and went to the cinema or a dance hall. On one really big outing we hired a coach and went down to Bournemouth to play football. My own part in the day was nothing special – I was sick on the way down and sick on the way back, but then I have never liked going on coaches.

The highlight of the day came when we were ready to leave Bournemouth and go home, but we couldn't find one of the lads. He'd gone off drinking, and first of all we didn't know where he was and then we couldn't get him back to the coach. He was completely plastered. We were supposed to leave at eleven o'clock and it was half-past twelve before we got going. Back in Lambourn he went off with some girl and we didn't see him again for a few hours – until he turned up to ride work next morning still wearing his suit. He had woken up to find it was too late to go back to his digs and get his jodhpurs and boots, so there he was a few minutes later flying across the top of the Downs on one of his Governor's horses still wearing his best clothes. The exercise probably cured his hangover but it can't have done his whistle much good.

What I remember most about those days is the laughs we had. And the pleasure of working at a job that everyone enjoyed. We happened to have a great bunch of lads when I was an apprentice, and after a couple of years there were few things outside racing that anyone in our stable would have wanted to do.

ESPECIALLY WHEN YOU LAUGH

You do get apprentices and lads who go out of racing for six months or a year. Then, as often as not, they come back again. Racing is a way of life. They come back not just for the horses, they come back for the whole deal: to be wet, cold and penniless, having blown their pay at cards on Friday night or from betting on horses at the weekend and having to borrow for the rest of the week. Unsocial hours, primitive housing, no privacy, lousy pay – they come back for all that. They must do, because they know that these things are inseparable from the good things – the excitement of the work, the nice people you meet, the fact that you never have to wait long before you can have a laugh. All right, it may not be the life for everyone, but it suited us fine and the laughs made up for the rest. Easily.

HOW TO BUY A JUMPER

Before The Sales – Who Is Looking For What, And What They Settle For

Fortunately, it's like women. If all men liked the same kind of woman, then 98% of the female population would be without a husband.

Suppose, instead of going to a horse sale, I went to a fashion show at which I was able to buy the model of my choice. The first girls come on and I think they are all absolutely stunning. To judge from their response, so do quite a few other members of the audience. But now another factor comes into it. Much as I admire each of these girls, I soon realize from the programme notes that they are out of my price range. I must look elsewhere.

I wait, and my patience is rewarded. Further down the list is a girl I can afford. She is quite good-looking too; one leg is a bit wonky, but I don't mind that; when I get her home I may be able to sort that out. I put in my bid, and a sale is made.

It's the same with horses. If I went to a horse sale with an open cheque book, I could pick out and buy the horse I most liked the look of. It would have good conformation, be well bred, everything about it would be special. I would then offer to pay x pounds for it (x million pounds nowadays) and the horse would be mine. But let's say I don't have quite that much money – and someone else does. I have to wait for the next batch. On they come: they're nice-looking animals; they move well, even if they aren't quite as well bred as the first ones I saw. The only problem is, they are out of my price range too. On to the next batch. These are even less well-bred; out of the two horses I quite like, one has a dam who never won a race, although *her* dam had a few successes. The other horse has a wall-eye, but that is not something that worries me. There is also the question of age.

As some racegoers know, and many do not, all horses have their 1st birthday on the 1st January following the year of their birth. Obviously, those born in January, February and March have a considerable start over horses born in, say, May or June. In its first year a foal is a foal until the 1st January, regardless of when in the year it was born and then it becomes a yearling; one year later it becomes a two-year-old.

There are prospective owners who care very much about those first few months of a foal's life, and would like all their foals to be foals for a minimum of eleven months and three and a half weeks. Others are more relaxed about it. 'I don't mind a late foal,' they say, 'I'll give it a bit more time.'

It's a good thing for the horse population that prospective owners hold such a wide variety of views, and possess such a wide variety of bank balances. If they did not, some horses would never have a home to go to. As it is, nearly every animal put into a yearling sale somehow finds a new owner. They may not find a buyer at the sale, but somehow or other they will be out there next year racing as two-year-olds. It beats me what happens to them all. Sometimes, I know, the runt of the litter is put into a sale and no-one wants to buy it. It may be the apple of the owner's eye – the chap who bred it – but that means nothing to the others. The owner puts a reserve of so-much on it, no-one makes a bid and the owner ends up taking the horse home again. Next he persuades Joe Bloggs down the road to train it for half-price and a share in the horse. Right. That's the little horse taken care of.

And off they all go again – breeding, training, selling, buying, hoping. The search for future winners is a never-ending, very expensive, maddening lottery. No matter how much a prospective owner spends, he can never be sure. There are no guarantees. Horses whose fine breeding suggests they are cast-iron certainties, may turn out to be hopeless on the racetrack. Not long ago someone spent $13.1 million on a horse which was so unsuited to racing it was never even entered. At the other end of the scale, people are breeding from horses which are such no-hopers, they really shouldn't be allowed. And yet, you never quite know. Every now and again, an animal which was useless as a racehorse goes and produces a foal which totally defies its background and wins a Classic. As long as there is that faint chance of big-time success, there is never any shortage of people willing to stake their cash – and lots of it.

But if a horse's pedigree is not a totally reliable indicator of its quality, what is? Well, you can tell a certain amount from its appearance, the way it looks and moves, though here, of course, we are entering a different kind of territory, an unpredictable world of personal preferences and prejudices. I will give you some examples.

For myself, I like an animal with a nice head. Horses come into the winner's enclosure in all shapes and sizes, but it's very seldom you find a horse in there that doesn't have a nice head. By that I mean it will have sharp, well-defined features, ears that aren't small (big ears are said to be a sign of generosity), and a nice big eye (indicating a kind nature) with not a lot of white surrounding it, big nostrils, and a generally alert look.

To me, eyes reveal a lot about character and potential – in both humans and animals. A man applying for a job may have the best qualifications in the world, or a horse the best pedigree, but if

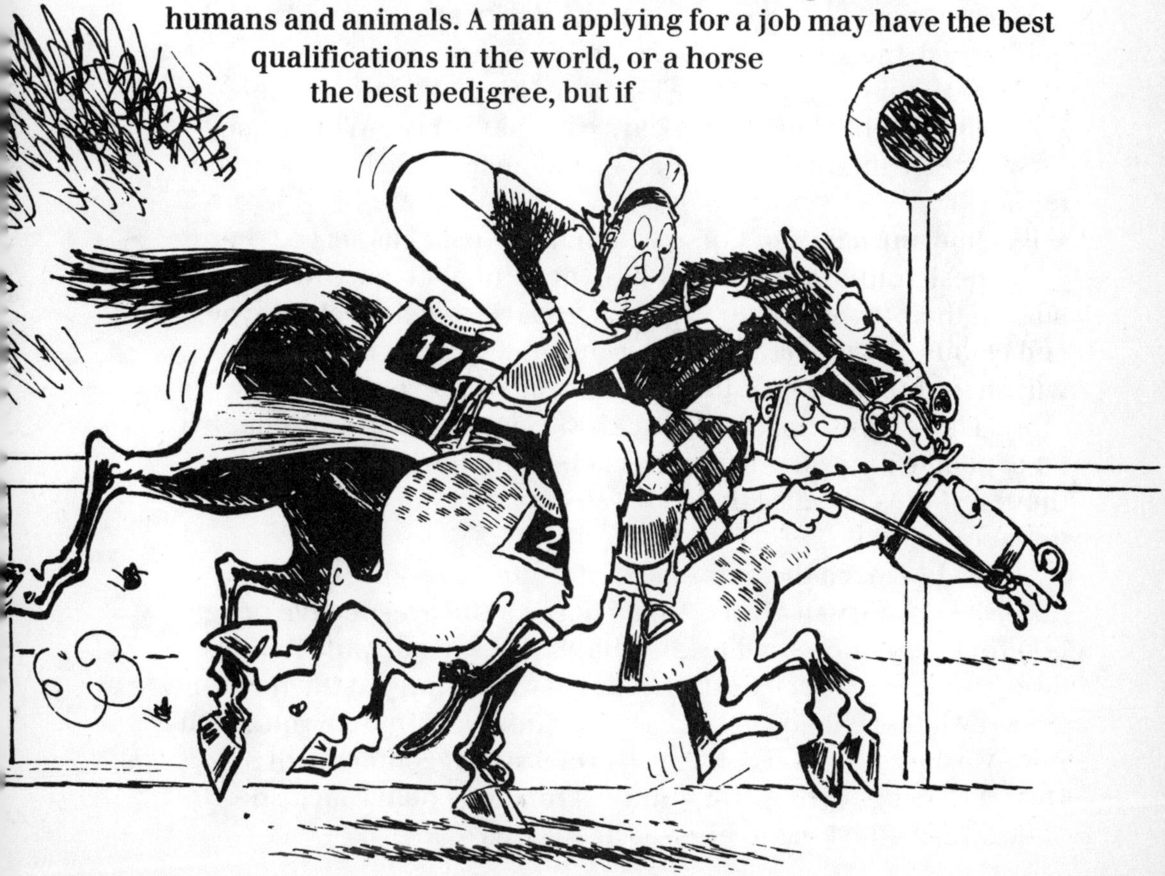

they don't look at you right you can bet they aren't interested in what you have in mind for them, and you might as well not start. Nine times out of ten you will be wasting your time.

So the head is important, the eyes in particular. For some people, it is the overall shape and size which count most. Small horses are popular with a number of trainers, and for reasons which make a lot of sense. Small horses stay sound for longer because they don't have so much weight to bear, and are less likely to break down or develop tendon trouble.

Going further, you can spot the preferences of individual trainers. Tim Forster, for example. If I walked down to the start at Newbury, I would not need a racecard to pick out Tim Forster's horse. It would be a big chestnut: strong, with big limbs and big everything. That's how he likes them.

Mercy Rimell likes a smart-looking dark bay horse with black points on it, the kind of animal that seems just right for a middleweight hunter-class. That is her kind of horse. Fulke Walwyn loves big horses, big bays especially. Fred Winter goes for a slightly smaller type of horse, and he too nearly always goes for bays.

By choosing a type of horse which in the past has served them well, these trainers, and many like them, hope to narrow the odds in their favour. They won't necessarily exclude other types and colours, a grey or a black, for instance, but their preference will be for the big bay or the chestnut, or whatever they fancy most. There is little prejudice against certain colours, although a lot of people are wary of very light chestnut horses, especially if they are fillies because they have a reputation for being temperamental.

A grey horse, on the other hand, despite belonging to a minority group, will always find a home if the prospective buyer is sufficiently impressed by the quality of its head, build and movement. One of the best 'chasers in the country at the moment is a grey horse called Desert Orchid. There's nothing wrong with him. Most people who come into professional contact with Desert Orchid never see anything of him except his backside.

Now that's the kind of horse that appeals to me.

RAIN, MUD, HAIL AND SUNSHINE

When The Going Gets Tough . . .

With the winters we have in this country, I often wonder why people bother to train jumping horses. Some years you can get two months when there's no racing at all. That's when things begin to fall apart.

After a week or two of being laid off, the jockeys are getting noticeably fat. If they don't ruin themselves through idleness, they go off skiing and break an arm. Then the trainer sees his chance and sneaks off for a quick holiday. The lads have to be there all the time, of course, looking after the horses, but then they always do.

The days go by and there's a lot of looking out the window and wondering what to do next. It must break soon, the trainer says to himself, so we'll just keep the horses going. If racing starts again next week, we've got to be ready for it. The weather doesn't change and next week's racing is off as well. This isn't good for the horses because they have been brought to the point of being ready to race, but have nowhere to go and do it.

Then at last the freeze shows signs of ending. There's enough of a thaw to get racing restarted and you send your horse off to run; but the weather turns colder the night before and the meeting is abandoned. You bring the horse home and send it off somewhere else; that's abandoned too.

Now it is all getting quite difficult and you wonder what to do about it. Plan A hasn't worked, and nor has Plan B. All right, you can go on devising back-up plans till the cows come home. The trouble is, each new plan tends to be that little bit weaker than the one before. Plan A was the best: the horse was down to run at the right moment on ground which suited it. When that meeting was called off, you sent the horse somewhere else although you knew the conditions weren't going to suit it quite as much. It's even worse with the third-choice meeting, because you know full well that the conditions aren't going to suit it at all. Well, you say to yourself, if we don't run it now it may not get another chance for a long time; the weather could easily get worse again. The horse runs, and does badly, then the weather comes good. The sun shines for a week; if only you'd waited, you could have run it when it stood a decent chance.

But then, supposing the weather doesn't come good. Instead of sunshine it snows hard for the next three weeks and you can't get any of your horses out. In that case, you have done the right thing because you ran it and took a chance. Neither you nor the owner is over the moon about the result, but at least you tried.

In another of these winter scenarios, racing has restarted but the frost hasn't quite come out of the ground, and you are in two minds about running the horse. You would prefer to send it, but you resent having to spend all that money on transport for nothing. On the other hand, the owner has been out to all the abandoned meetings and he is pissed off with getting no action. You decide to run it, not just to keep the owner happy but because you think it will be good for the horse. On the day, the going is that little bit harder than you wanted. The horse breaks down. So then who's happy? No-one.

Here are some signs to look out for when you next go racing. If you remember these basic points, you will nearly always be able to tell which sort of ground a horse prefers, and whether it will be good on soft ground or hard. Once you are able to assess this, you can adjust your betting accordingly and you will be able to enjoy your racing that much more.

The secret is in the galloping movement. The way a horse gallops is a sure indicator of the type of ground it likes to travel over and, therefore, the ground on which it will perform best.

A horse that gallops with a circular, churning action, the legs pounding round and round, is a horse that likes soft ground. Its hooves are hitting the ground very hard, so it benefits from a softer, muddy top which it can pull itself through without jarring itself and getting injured. When this horse can feel that the ground is soft, it is more confident about going faster. It thinks it can't hurt itself and so it doesn't mind trying a bit harder.

A horse that gallops with a more flowing, sweeping action, throwing its legs out in front, is a horse that likes firm ground. At its best, this horse moves forward smoothly and sweetly, bouncing lightly off the ground at each contact. But as soon as it meets soft ground it tends to get lost. Its feet can't bounce and instead they go in too far, which alters the rhythm and slows down the pace.

Another type to watch out for is the horse with big feet. Will this do better or worse on soft ground? Think about it for a moment, before you read on.

I can understand why people get this wrong, because they think a horse with big feet will sink in further and not be able to travel forward as well as a horse with small feet. In fact the reverse is true, the reason being that the horse with big feet is able to spread its weight over a larger area of ground and this reduces the tendency to sink into it. There's a human comparison here between someone wearing flat shoes and someone in high heels: it's the one in the high heels who is going to get stuck in soft or muddy ground, whereas the one in the boats doesn't have this problem and just carries on moving forward.

TWICE LUCKY

Now, here's another pointer which might seem to conflict with what I have just been saying. If you have a race over soft ground between two three-year-olds, and one is a great big horse and the other a small wiry animal, the small wiry animal will usually do better. This is because, at that age, the big horse will not have finished growing. Although it is big, it is still comparatively weak and therefore liable to tire more quickly in soft or wet conditions. Part of this horse's diet is still going into making it grow to its full size, whereas the little horse has already grown as big as it is going to be, and all its food is going towards improving its health and strength.

Hard ground is something else. The horse I described earlier, the one with the sweeping, floating action, will do well on firm ground, but this is very different from hard ground. Very few horses like galloping on hard ground and the reason for this is very simple: it hurts and it's dangerous.

If you look back at the form-books of just two years ago, and see how many of those horses are still running today, you will get an idea of the breakdown rate among jumping horses. Even in the best conditions it is asking a lot of a horse to gallop and jump, and on hard ground the stresses and strains are that much worse. Horses can't stand it; their tendons go and they either have to rest for a year or they are finished as steeplechasers.

You watch a horse when it lands after jumping a fence. Its front legs are subjected to a terrific strain as half a ton of bodyweight bears down on them. The shock hits in the area of the fetlock and travels up into the tendon. This can only stand so much stress, and when it packs up the horse can't race again without prolonged rest and possibly an operation as well.

The wastage among jumping horses is probably the worst aspect of the whole sport. It's almost criminal the way the stables run through so many horses – good, capable animals which do their best in training, last for a few races and then break down through no fault of their own, simply because they are being asked to do something for which they are not naturally built. Horses were made to gallop, but not to gallop and jump. They *can* do it, we know, but in asking them to run at full speed and jump a series of fences in between, we are stretching them to the limit of their physical capabilities.

Some horses are really tough and go on until they are fourteen or sixteen, but the vast majority suffer an injury of one kind or another within two, three or four years. Once that has happened, it is likely to happen again, so even if a horse makes a full recovery its chances of continuing for long as a jump horse are very limited.

There are plenty of less strenuous things they can do when their racing days are over. In racing it is the speed at which the jumping is done that causes the damage. Going at a more relaxed pace, an ex-jumper can go into showjumping or three-day eventing and do well; or it can start a new life as a hack or a hunter, even jumping at point-to-point meetings where everything goes a lot slower.

And how about the jockeys? Do the weather and the state of the ground affect the way they do their job? Well, in theory, perhaps they should not. A jockey should be impervious to such things; waterproof in body and soul against the worst freezing fog and the most biting hailstorm. All the same, I can tell you, there are times when even a jockey exhibits human failings.

Not long before I finished riding, I had this difficult horse to school. It was a really expensive horse which had come second in the Derby and then went on to hurdling. It could jump all right, but some days it just didn't want to; it was one of those awkward animals – and on this particular morning we had the weather to match the horse's temperament. It was very wet and very cold. One minute driving rain was slashing across the gallops, cutting into our faces, and when this went off it was followed by those icy gusts of wind which can tear the heart out of a jockey at that hour of the morning, especially if he is feeling sorry for himself anyway.

I was feeling sorry for myself. It was two days after the Cheltenham Festival meeting. I hadn't had a winner, and knew I wouldn't be racing much longer. I got on this horse in the freezing rain, and all it wanted to do was prove to me that it had a

13

mind of its own. To start with, it would not jump. It stopped at every hurdle. I wasn't in the mood, as I have said, but I stuck at the job and after a while I got the horse jumping. Success. Hmm, maybe. With some horses there is nothing you can take for granted.

We jumped another hurdle and were going along quite nicely when all of a sudden the horse dug its toes in and, for the last time in our working relationship, stopped. It did it so quickly, I was caught out and my wrists were badly jarred as they snapped forward. I have a plate in my left arm from an earlier accident when I broke my arm, and the shock of this horse stopping was very painful. Add to this the bad mood I had been in ever since Cheltenham, plus the terrible weather. The combination of all three made something go in my head. I got off the horse, gave it a kick in the belly, stamped over to my car, got in it and drove home without a word.

Later, I 'phoned the trainer and apologized, and was forgiven. Even so, looking back, I am convinced it was the worst display of bad temper I have ever come across in my racing career. Blame it on what you like, the evil weather must have had *something* to do with it.

RACING TYPES

The Clothes They Wear And The Cars They Drive

There must be a kind of herd instinct which affects people when they go racing. You keep seeing them in groups. Owners with other owners and their mates; jockeys with other jockeys; punters in a gang on the train, bookies in a long line at the course. It's one group after another. Another funny thing is how they often look alike, dress alike and drive the same cars.

Though not always, as we shall see.

TRAINERS

Trainers are the most varied-looking people in racing. What they want most of all is to be lucky, and so as long as it doesn't look too horrible they will go on wearing the same suit or coat which they were wearing the last time they had a winner. Day after day they turn out in the same old gear, and the excuse they give for doing this is that it makes them easier to recognize.

Now you know the real reason why David Nicholson wears red socks every time he goes to the races, and one of those sheepskin coats which looks like it's inside out, with seams of sheepskin poking out of the suede. Henry Cecil is more unconventional than most. He is one of a tiny number of men in the paddock who don't wear a trilby; what's more, he doesn't carry binoculars, and he usually chooses trousers in some loud colour like custard-yellow. Rodney Simpson, who trains at Lambourn, likes to wear a leather suit, either brown or yellow or green, and quite often a mixture of all three. Rodney Simpson is what you would call a bright dresser.

Around these very visible people you get the other trainers who dress in average, once-smart country clothes – tweed suits, cord trousers, brogue shoes, racing coats and Husky jackets. They are the kind of outfits that many other people wear, the only difference being that trainers never like to send theirs to the cleaners in case they break some magic chain of luck. It's all total nonsense, of course, but they like to believe it.

JOCKEYS

Not so very long ago it would have been unthinkable for a jockey not to wear a suit to the races. Nowadays, unless it is a big Saturday meeting, most jump jockeys turn up in a pair of jeans and a sweater.

In a way it is more sensible for a jockey to wear casual clothes. When he gets to the races he goes into the weighing room and changes into his racing gear. As far as weighing rooms are concerned, the clothes-hanger has yet to be invented, so the jockeys hang their everyday clothes on pegs. Fellow jockeys in a hurry brush them off and they usually end up in the wet and mud on the floor.

The only other reason for wearing a suit is if the jockey is invited to have a drink with one of the owners. When I was riding I was never into going round the bars, so wearing a suit, plus a clean shirt and tie, had very little attraction for me.

People are more down to earth than they used to be, and that goes for jockeys too. In the old days, if it was very cold or raining hard a jockey would walk out to the paddock wearing a coat over his colours. When the time came to mount, the travelling head lad would take the coat from him. You never see that nowadays; jockeys reckon that they are going to get cold and wet anyway, so a couple of minutes in the paddock will make no difference.

... AND THE CARS THEY DRIVE

When it comes to choosing a car, professional racing people are seized by group mania. A survey of who owns what would reveal that three makes of car completely dominate the racing scene. They are Mercedes, Audi and BMW. All German, all powerful cars, all chosen because they have a big reputation for covering long distances with a minimum of hassle.

In that narrow range you also find some even narrower categories of loyalty. Most trainers, jumping and flat, drive an Audi, a small Mercedes or a 3- or 5-series BMW. Most of the top flat jockeys drive a big Mercedes, but only the very top flat trainers get to this level. The less successful flat jockeys drive 3- or 5-series BMWs or a Toyota Celica or something similar.

The demands of the racing calendar almost force trainers and jockeys into buying the most reliable, most comfortable and reasonably speedy car they can afford. The evidence of which cars they prefer will give little comfort to British manufacturers.

OWNERS AND SMART SPECTATORS

Jump-racing is a sort-of poor relation to the flat. By this I mean that the owners of jumping horses and their friends are not

exactly poor, but you don't see the extremes of dress or behaviour that you find at the big flat-race meetings.

There is a difference, for instance, between a Newbury flat meeting and a Newbury jump meeting. At the flat meeting you will see six times more Rolls Royces in the car park and ten times more Mercedes. You will see more Porsches, more Mercedes with the AMG conversion and various other types of exotic car, and the reason is that flat meetings like this one, also Royal Ascot and others near London attract a much richer, flashier type of person. The fast boys from the City come down, for instance, and they don't know what to drink if it isn't in a bottle which goes 'Pop!' when they open it.

On the other hand, I would not say that jump people were less smart than the flat crowd. They *are* smart, but in their own way. The farmer who comes down from somewhere like Wincanton can be as smart as anybody who goes racing. He drives a fairly new Range Rover, or a Rover 90 or Volvo, and wears good, fairly expensive country clothes – and shoes that you can see your face in. For him and his wife, the lady in the Hermès scarf, Puffa jacket and tweed skirt, a day at the races is a special occasion and they enjoy putting on their best outdoor clothes to match the importance of the day (unlike the trainer for whom it is just another day, and anyway these are his lucky trousers).

THE MEN ON THE TRAIN

These are the comedians of the racing game. Their stamping grounds are the racecourses they can get to by train from London. Any morning of the week you will see them, fag in mouth, racing paper projecting from a jacket pocket, piling onto trains at Charing Cross, London Bridge or Victoria and heading off to Folkestone, Plumpton, Fontwell, etc.

They play cards on the way down, cards on the way home and they talk about nothing but horses and racing. What's going to win on the way there, why something got beaten on the way back. It's always the jockey's or somebody else's fault, never because their judgment was in any way faulty. They are not professional gamblers, just blokes who like to go racing once a week or whenever they are free. A typical punter like this may have a small cash business, perhaps a market stall, and this provides the money to keep him going and the freedom to enjoy himself with his mates.

At the course they add a lot of character to the meeting. When a fancied horse gets beaten, they are the ones who crowd round jeering and giving the jockey stick on the way in. 'What d'you leave it too late for?' they want to know, and 'Next time hit it properly, will ya.' I remember a jockey at Plumpton who had to stay in the weighing room until the last trainload of these boys had gone back to London. He'd been beaten on the favourite and they had gone mad. A policeman had to be put on special guard duty at the weighing room door to stop all these characters from getting in. I am not sure they would have done much damage, but they were definitely overheated and still had a lot of shouting left in them.

If you have any doubt about recognizing this type of racegoer, he wears a fairly clean shirt, dark blue pinstripe suit with maybe a red flower in his buttonhole, and dirty brown shoes. Don't ask me why, but he always neglects his shoes even if he is otherwise perfectly respectable-looking. He smokes a lot, either cigarettes or small cigars, drinks light ale and reads *The Sporting Life* and *The Sun*. You never see him read anything more serious than the tabloids – and no-one loves his racing more.

SAFETY FIRST

Jockeys Reckon To Fall Once Every Ten Races – Drunk or Sober

The most important consideration for a jump jockey is safety. Falls are an unavoidable part of the job and statistics show that a jockey can expect to fall about once every tenth race. The trick here is to avoid bad falls, to be able to get up and ride in the next race, and maybe win it. When you are lying in hospital, you aren't riding any winners at all – and that can hurt more than the injury.

Sometimes there is nothing you can do about it. If you come off in front of twenty other horses, it is entirely in God's hands whether they all miss you, or trample all over you.

You curl up in a ball if you can, and wait. It usually takes just a couple of seconds for the rest of the field to come by, though it feels like ten minutes. In a race at Wincanton I had fallen in front of a big field. I lay there all rolled up on the ground, hoping and praying that nothing would stand on me or kick me as it came past. There were fifteen other runners in that race, and when they had all gone by I thanked my lucky stars and went to stand up. Just then, the horse that had thrown me got to its feet about five yards away and came and galloped all over me, cracking two of my ribs. It could have gone in any direction it liked in a space of about two hundred acres – and it chose to come and flatten me.

Another day, at Huntingdon, I thought I had got away with a fall. All the other horses came sweeping past, leaving me untouched. Thank God for that, I thought. Not quite all the others, however. As I started to get to my feet, a straggler came up, with a jockey on it, and trod all over me; it broke my collarbone.

I like to think that a professional jockey would have missed me, because in various ways the pros try to look after each other. They also have the ability to know what is going on and deal with an emergency such as this. Unfortunately, at Huntingdon, it was not to be; the rider was an amateur and it showed.

The trouble with most amateurs is that they don't get enough practice. A race day is their big day out; they don't watch what they are doing because they are too fascinated watching everybody else. As well as being less skilful at riding, they go round in a kind of daze which gets worse towards the end of a race because they are not fit and nor is their horse. It's no wonder they have accidents.

In those situations, and in others like them, the jockey who has a fall is powerless to influence his fate. But there are other ways in which he can improve his chances of avoiding injury. Starting with the horses he rides.

When a jockey takes out a horse and starts jumping it for the first time, he is looking to see whether it is a natural jumper or whether it is some other kind of animal. The natural jumper finds it easy to do; it has a natural spring and a smooth movement, and when it doesn't meet a fence in exactly the right stride it is able to put in a short stride and adjust its position before take-off. During the jump it has the sense to keep its feet away from the obstacle, and as it lands and runs on it is able to grasp what is happening in front of it and instinctively cope with what needs to be done. This includes taking avoiding action, which some horses can do and some can't. Partly this is a matter of being alert, and partly it's having the nimbleness to get past,

say, a fallen horse which is lying in its path only a stride away. The difference between success and failure may only be about as wide as one hair on a horse's tail, but time and again you get one horse which succeeds and another which can't quite make it.

If a horse doesn't have those natural qualities, the jockey is the first to find out. It may jump perfectly well as long as it is able to meet every fence and hurdle on the right stride. The test comes not so much when it has to stand off a little bit farther but when it has to come in close and fiddle with its stride pattern. If it isn't nimble enough to sort this out for itself, and get it right, the jockey is in trouble.

How nice it is, therefore, when a jockey gets on a horse and finds he is riding a natural jumper, bright, quick-thinking and nimble. It's a special feeling.

But let's not blame it all on the horse. Sometimes a jockey can be his own worst enemy. The one thing that makes horses fall quicker than anything else is indecision on the part of the jockey. Each time he goes into a fence, the jockey must make his mind up, and the horse's mind, about where they need to take off. If he hesitates, or leaves too much to the horse, that's when it will start jumping badly.

A horse can do a certain amount by itself in a jump, but it needs firm guidance to complete the job. If you look at the height of an average fence or hurdle and compare it with the distance between the ground and the bottom of a horse's stomach, you will see that the horse is half to three-quarters the way there quite naturally. It doesn't, therefore, have to make a great deal of effort to get itself over the fence.

When things go wrong, it is often because the jockey has made an error and caused the horse to lose confidence. If a jockey gives his horse a kick in the belly to take off from a point where it can't possibly clear the fence, the horse will immediately be confused; it will lose confidence both in itself and the jockey, and will start making blunders.

Sometimes the public don't appreciate how big a contribution the jockey makes. If they read something about Peter Scudamore being a safe jockey who has relatively few falls, they tend to say, 'Oh, well, it's all right for him, he's riding good horses which jump well.' In fact, the main reason these horses jump well is that Peter is a good jockey who knows what he is doing and passes his confidence on to the horses he rides. Another reason is that he is riding for good trainers who keep their horses fit so they race well and don't tire and make mistakes, especially towards the end of a race.

Another way a jockey can keep his good health is not to ride for the wrong sort of trainer. Some people find it hard to believe that they exist, but there are trainers who not only don't school their horses properly, they will even send a horse to a jump race when it has only jumped one fence in its life, if that. Not surprisingly, these trainers have more fallers than anyone else and good jockeys steer well clear of them.

There is a story about a jockey who was asked to ride a horse in a novice 'chase at Bangor. The trainer was well known as one of the dodgiest around, so the jockey refused. 'Sorry,' he said, 'but it's Liverpool next week – the Grand National.'

'Oh,' said the trainer, and went off to try and book someone else.

At Aintree the following week, just before the start of the National, the trainer found himself standing next to this same jockey.

'Here,' said the trainer, 'when I asked you to ride my horse last week, I thought you said no because you had a ride in the Grand National.'

'No,' said the jockey, 'I just wanted to watch the race from here – and not from a hospital bed.'

He meant it, too, and I know how he must have felt. My biggest fall was in that race, when the horse in front pulled up at Becher's Brook and mine couldn't jump the fence. It stopped, but we were so close to the fence that I was whipped over the top and fell, backwards, about fourteen feet into the ditch. Not something I would care to repeat. And that was on a good horse.

Sometimes it looks worse than it really is. A friend of mine had a fall one day at Wye, near Folkestone. Three riders fell at the same fence; the other two were all right and picked themselves up, but this other fellow was still on the ground, unconscious.

When they got over to him his body was convulsing and they immediately thought that he must be seriously hurt. Then a closer look showed what had really happened. He had been thrown over the running rail onto the inside of the racecourse

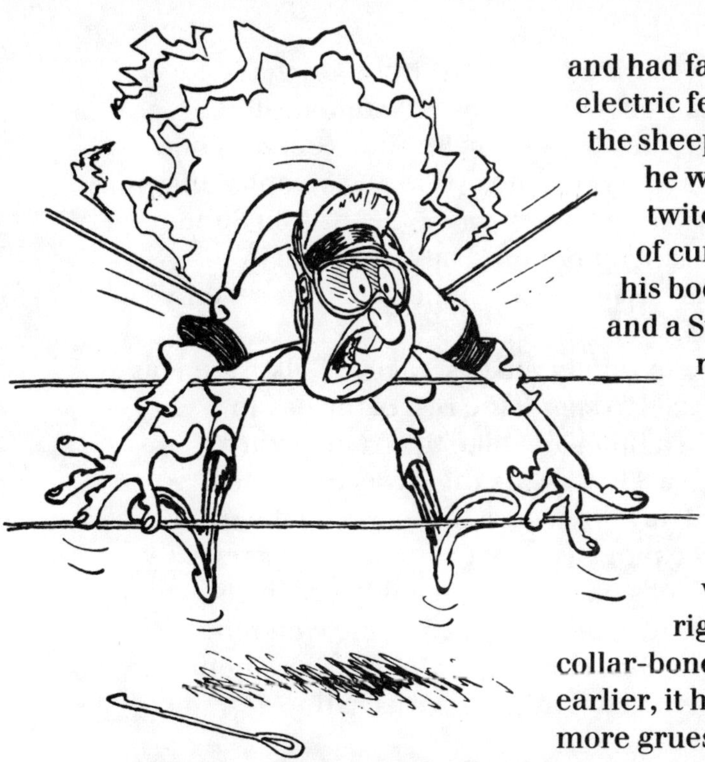

and had fallen across an electric fence put there to keep the sheep in. Every two seconds he was giving a horrible twitch as another burst of current passed through his body. The jockeys and a St John Ambulance man pulled him off the wire – carefully timing their efforts so that they too didn't get a shock – and he came round and was more or less all right with just a broken collar-bone. A couple of minutes earlier, it had all looked a lot more gruesome.

Every so often a jockey's nightmare comes true. In 1987 it happened to Richard Rowe. He fell in the last race, but it was getting dark by then and nobody noticed. All the other jockeys went off to the weighing room to get changed and he was left out there. It was a long time before somebody said, 'Where's Richard?'

When they found him, he was lying by one of the fences with a broken leg. It was definitely not his lucky day because by then the ambulance had gone home, so poor Richard had a very nasty wait until he could get some proper medical treatment. It was just one of those things. It even seems quite funny when you tell it as a story – unless, that is, you have ever been the one who got left behind.

Just once in a while a jockey has a fall and feels no pain. This is quite a rare phenomenon but it did happen to Johnny Haine. He and Jeff King went up to Ayr for a meeting. They flew up on the Thursday and that night went out and enjoyed themselves. They rode on the Friday and celebrated in the evening. On the Saturday they each had a ride in the Scottish National, after which they planned to fly back to London for the evening. Then someone asked them to a party and they went and sampled the good Scottish hospitality. As a result it was some time on Sunday afternoon before they reached London. They were still in reasonable shape despite having been on the booze for seventy-two hours.

Both men were booked to ride in the first race at Folkestone on the Monday, so they decided to spend the rest of the day in London, stay overnight in a hotel and take the train down to Folkestone in the morning. They drank their way through Sunday evening and next day they had a few more on the train.

At the racecourse they changed and went out for their race. By now they were as full as ticks but just about able to get on a horse. When the race was over Jeff returned to the weighing room and looked round for John but couldn't find him. Then someone said he had fallen at the third and was in the ambulance room.

Jeff went round there straight away and found John lying on one of the beds. 'Come on,' he said, 'hurry up or we'll miss the early train.'

Then the doctor came over. 'This man can't be moved,' he said. 'There may be something seriously wrong with him.'

'What do you mean?' said Jeff. 'What's the matter with him?'

'Well,' said the doctor, 'it's lucky I saw this but I happened to be standing at the hurdle where he fell. As he hit the ground he was violently sick, so now we are keeping him in for observation.'

'What!' said Jeff. 'Of course he was sick. *You'd* be sick if you'd drunk all he's had in the last four days!'

The doctor glared at John. 'Drink,' he said, 'you didn't tell me you had been drinking.'

'You didn't ask me,' said John. 'But I told you I was all right really.'

So then, while the doctor had a bit of a fit, Jeff dragged John out of the room and they disappeared as fast as they could. No point in causing a scene and getting the stewards involved.

TRAVELLING MEN

Here Today, Folkestone Tomorrow – Jockeys And Trainers Do More Travelling Than Any Other Competitors in Sport

When Tommy Carmody, the great Irish jockey, came over to live in England, he was based up in the North with Michael Dickinson. The first time he came south was to race at Huntingdon. He arranged to have a lift down with Jonjo O'Neill and Ron Barry.

They met at a service station on the M6 and Jonjo and Ron said, 'Tell you what, Tommy, you drive halfway and we'll drive the rest.'

Tommy agreed and they set off. They had been going for about two hours when Tommy asked if they were nearly halfway there.

'No, no, not yet, Tommy,' said the other two, nodding slyly to each other. 'Bit more yet.'

On he drove, and then a bit more. An hour and a half later, they got Tommy to pull into the side of the A1 and announced that it was time for a change of driver. Tommy looked at his watch, did some quick sums and said, 'Look, fellers, we'll be late, won't we?'

Jonjo and Ron shook their heads. 'That'll be all right, Tommy,' they said. 'We'll get there in time.'

Ron Barry moved over to the driver's seat. Two miles down the road, he pulled off the A1 and drove into the racecourse.

Still, at least Tommy got there. Another time, he was due to

travel south with Jonjo and Ron to race at Ascot. Unfortunately, Tommy went and waited on the northbound side of the M6 while the others were looking all over the other side of the road for him. In the end I think he had to drive himself – which he was getting quite used to by then.

There is a tailpiece to that story which involves me – not directly with Tommy, but I was once in a situation quite like the one where he was being made to do all the driving. There are at least two reasons why I shouldn't repeat this story and the solution that I came up with. For one thing it has appeared in print several times already and, for another, I wouldn't like anyone else to try it out for themselves as it is what some people might consider dangerous.

Now you have been warned, I will get on with the story. We were coming back from Devon & Exeter one day, when I decided I had done enough driving. I had driven all the way down there,

had six rides, and coming back on the M4 I tried to get somebody else to take over from me, but the other three didn't want to know.

'Come on,' I said, 'it wouldn't hurt one of you to take us the rest of the way back.'

In the back seat were Colin Brown and Philip Blacker, and sitting next to me was Nicky Henderson. They were warm and comfortable and didn't want to move. Nobody said anything.

'Right,' I said. The car was one of those Fiats which was fitted with a cruise control. I pulled it on and climbed into the back of the car. So now we were going along the motorway at about seventy miles an hour with nobody in the driver's seat. That put a little bit of pressure on Nicky, who was nearest to the steering wheel, and after he'd recovered from his surprise, he slipped across behind the wheel and drove us back home. Nice chap, Nicky.

It is unusual for a jockey to go racing by himself. Most of the time we would find out the day before who was going where and decide who to share a car with. I have this slight peculiarity in that I get car-sick if I'm not driving, so I usually ended up doing most of the driving, either in my own car or someone else's, and we split the petrol between us.

I have found, by the way, that I don't feel car-sick in the front passenger seat if I can hold the steering wheel. Somehow, that way, I feel part of the car, not separately floating with that slight motion which gradually gets through to the stomach and makes your breakfast start hopping about. However, some jockeys aren't very keen on driving a car while there is a third hand on the steering wheel, so I tended to do more driving than most.

Andy Turnell told me about a time when he thought he had got his transport fixed up, but things didn't turn out as planned. He was racing at Warwick one day on one of his dad's horses. He got beaten, but his dad thought he should have won it. After the race the old man was so annoyed, he got in the car and drove straight off home, leaving Andy to travel back in the horsebox.

In Ireland they often have their own way of doing things. I was over there not long ago for a day's hunting. When we had finished, one of the people there couldn't fit all his horses into the horsebox. Somehow they kept jamming up at the back and leaving no room for the last two.

Then the owner thought of a plan. He got into the driving cab, started up the engine, drove off down the road and then smartly put the brakes on. All the horses inside the box shunted up to the front, just like a lot of commuters on a train, and then he had someone quickly lead up the other two horses and put them in the back.

It could only happen in Ireland.

ALL PART OF THE GAME

Jump Jockeys And Their Funny Ways

In jump racing there is no room for big-headed jockeys. Before a meeting, a jockey has much less idea than a flat jockey about what will happen to him. The rewards are similar, in that he may ride three winners and go home a happy man. The penalties, though, are much more varied and painful. Instead of three winners he may have three falls; instead of a quiet ride home he may leave the course in an ambulance.

The conditions in which they race are also a good deal more unpredictable. Jump racing is a winter sport and the weather alone – the freezing cold, the wringing wet – can be enough to keep a man fairly humble. It makes for a certain kind of camaraderie, a willingness to help each other and share problems, along with drinking the other bloke's champagne.

I don't want to go too far about this. Jump jockeys are only human after all, and the part of their trade they like most is riding winners. So, if you have a fall and hurt yourself, and are down to ride a good horse in the next race, you need not expect your mates to visit you in the ambulance room until they have dashed after your horse's trainer to see if they can ride it in your place. Then they'll come and see you. It's all part of the game.

Other people have written about the hardships inflicted on novice jockeys in the weighing room. Nothing I can say here will stop these childish practices, but I think you can learn a lot about the mentality of a group of men when you know how they like to amuse themselves – for instance, by getting someone to follow the new jockey out to the paddock and quietly pin a pair of girl's knickers on his back. There he is, poor little devil, talking solemnly to the owner about his horse while this lacy object is blowing in the breeze behind him. Senior jockeys, men with greying hair and grandchildren, actually think that kind of thing is funny.

Novice riders are not the only ones to suffer. The practical jokery is a constant hazard and no-one is safe. They will take a pair of scissors and cut the toes off your socks; or the 'Y' out of

your Y-fronts. They will snip the flybuttons off your trousers, or Superglue the soles of your shoes to the floor. If they aren't damaging each other's property, they are attacking each other mentally, dropping their trousers as they pass you on the motorway and that kind of thing.

Jump jockeys are great kidders, and nothing delights them more than to find someone who is a little bit gullible and can be led up the garden path. Some years ago Philip Blacker was one of their victims: a very good jockey but too easily inclined to believe things people told him. One day at Fontwell he rode a blinding race on a horse trained by Alex Kilpatrick. He did everything right and finished second. Afterwards, we came up to him one by one and said things like: 'Thought you could have ridden it better than that,' or 'Didn't do very well there, Phil.'

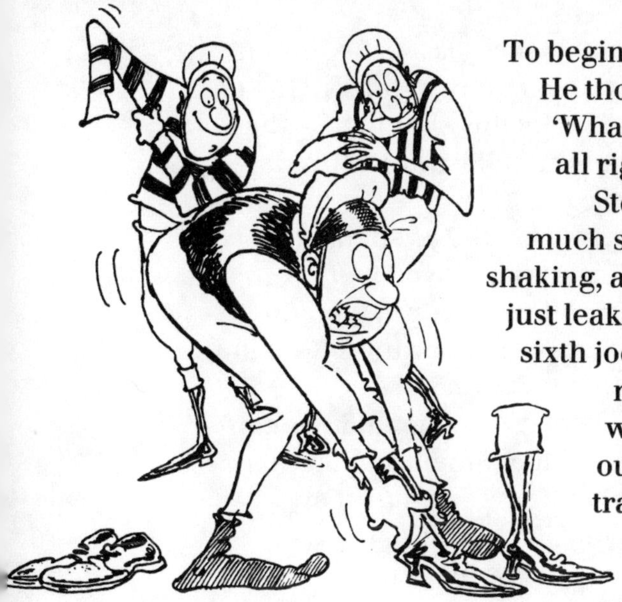

To begin with, he couldn't understand it. He thought he'd had a good race.

'What do you mean?' he said. 'I did all right.'

Steadily we worked on him, with much sucking of teeth and head-shaking, and steadily his self-confidence just leaked away. By the time the fifth or sixth jockey had told him he hadn't ridden the horse very well he was really confused – and went outside and apologized to the trainer!

Another victim was a young jockey who had just got himself a new pair of made-to-measure boots. He put them on in the corner one day and they fitted perfectly. He was obviously so pleased, he wanted other people to share his pleasure. He came over to me.

'What do you think of these, then?' he asked.

'They're great,' I said. 'Who were they made for?'

'What,' he said, looking surprised. 'They're for me. I just had them specially made.'

'No,' I said. 'They're much too long. They're about two inches too long for you.'

'Eh? Do you really think so?'

'Sure. You ought to have them seen to.'

He wasn't best pleased, so he went and asked someone else. Unfortunately for him, the joke was travelling round the weighing room quicker than he was. Everyone he asked said, 'Bit long, aren't they?' or 'Nice boots those. Shame you aren't a bit longer in the leg.' In the end he went off, poor chap, and had two inches cut off a pair of boots which fitted him immaculately.

Ordinary conversation among jump jockeys is a trifle limited. This is mainly because they only talk about two things. One of these is racing and the other is sex. Why this should be – the obsession with sex, I mean – is something I examine in a later chapter (entitled, appropriately, 'Sex').

Other topics of conversation are not barred as such, but it can be quite difficult to get a discussion started. If you were interested in politics or economics, or even money, you might say to someone, 'I can't see things getting better until Ronald Reagan sorts out their budget deficit.'

The reply of most jockeys would be, 'Who's Ronald Reagan?'

Those who didn't say that, would offer something like, 'Oh, yes. He's that guy who was an actor. I bet he screwed a lot of good-looking birds when he was in Hollywood.'

They can't help it. It's just the way they see things.

Every so often, jockeys do something which even other people find amusing. A few years back there was a jockey called Billy who didn't ride many winners but he always had an excuse. 'The going was wrong for it,' he'd say, or 'Too many runners. I had him just ready but I couldn't get him out.' It was either that or else somebody bumped him and it wasn't noticed, or he did get out but then he had too far to go round the outside. Whatever happened, it was never Billy's fault.

He died young, killed in a 'plane crash. At his funeral his fellow jockeys clubbed together and bought him a huge wreath. There was a card pinned to it. The message read: 'Boxed-in again, Billy.'

BEWARE THE INTELLIGENT HORSE

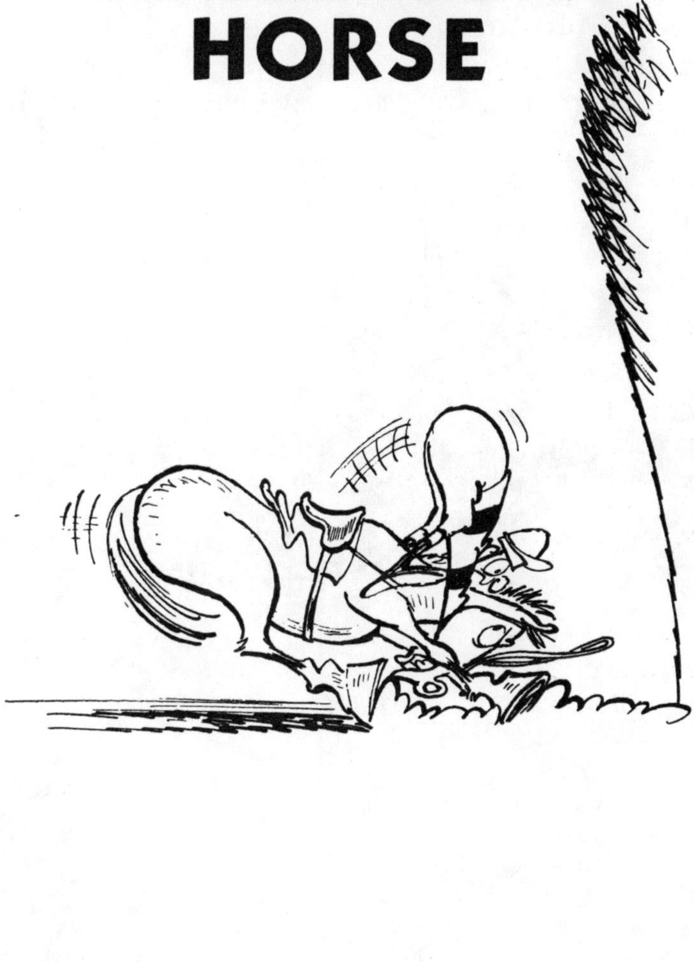

No Matter What The Stable Tries, Not All Horses Want To Go Faster

At my stables we used to break in a lot of yearlings. We bought them at the Sales, they came to us off the studs and our first job was to settle them down and break them in. But already their characters were formed. They were their own little people and, whatever you might try to do, they would change hardly at all.

The ones that were willing and worked hard to please you were like that from the word go. So were the ones who, if they

were human beings, would be described as borstal cases. The first week you have them, when you find all this out, is often a difficult time. By the end of it, you may wish you could send most of them back. Then, of course, it is too late.

All is not lost, however. Even with the one who looked bright and willing at the Sale, and then turns into a little horror – you can't get the bridle on it, you can't get the saddle on it, it doesn't want to go up the road . . . The trick is to get every new horse on your side as quickly as you can, so that it begins to enjoy the work it is being given to do and becomes more co-operative. Often you can succeed with a horse that was difficult to begin with. It grows into a good, tough animal which is well worth having.

Others are not so good. They decide, early on, that they don't like this running-about business. You have them up on the gallops a couple of times, and you may think you are getting somewhere with them; then they rebel. 'Blow this for a game of soldiers,' they seem to say, and give up. They simply do not want to run. You try everything to get them going, including blinkers, but that only makes them worse. These horses are professional non-starters, and the sooner they are off your hands, the better.

Horses, thank goodness, are all different from each other, and it's being able to tell what is going on in each individual horse's head that distinguishes the good trainer from the bad. It would be a mistake, for instance, to think that all horses benefit from lots of work. Some perform much better if, after they have reached a certain stage in their development, you only take them up to the gallops once a week. Some need to go up there every day, but it would be wrong to assume that just because you as the trainer have to be up and schooling every morning of the week, all the horses must do the same.

From getting to know them when they first come to you, you progress to finding out how a horse performs under racing conditions. By now the permutations of what it likes and doesn't like have really begun to pile up. After a race, when a horse hasn't done well, its trainer can have dozens of possibilities to reckon with. Was it because it doesn't like being in a bunch? Did it hold back because it doesn't like going through a gap? Perhaps it would do better running from the front? Was it the ground? Would it go better on soft ground? Was it the course? Some horses don't like left-handed courses. Or was it the jockey? Horses have their favourite jockeys, just like humans. Was the race too far for it? Was the race too good for it? Did it travel well? Has it been feeding all right? Perhaps it's just no good?

By the time the trainer has narrowed down some of these choices, the condition and potential of the horse may have changed. Then the trainer decides to try it out with four different jockeys, and it runs four different races, the only common factor being that it doesn't win any of them.

None of this is likely to influence my view that training horses is a lunatic way to earn a living!

When we talk about the character of a horse, we tend quite naturally to describe it as if it was human. We say it is brave, idle, determined, intelligent, and so on. That is fair enough, I suppose, because we don't have an alternative set of horsey adjectives with which to label them any better. But I am not convinced that some of the words we use at the moment are quite accurate enough.

Take intelligence, and the way we judge it in a horse. For a start, I don't think that horses are anywhere near as intelligent as many people like to make out. Why should they be? Their brains are a good bit smaller in proportion to ours, they don't talk much amongst themselves and there must be a very low limit on their powers of reasoning.

For the most part, a horse's brain works through a combination of instinct, observation and memory. You get the odd horse which somehow impresses you as being brighter and more aware than the others, but I can't see that this has anything to do with reasoning power. Or if it does, then it must operate in a very elementary way which you can't really compare with human intelligence.

This may cause a stir down at the gymkhanas, and in hunting circles as well, but anyone who thinks I am being insulting to horses or who fervently believes that their beloved Blackie could

win *Mastermind* if it wanted to, should ask themselves why the racing performance of horses never really improves. This is an established fact which many people find surprising, but the times set by horses over any distance you like to name have not improved much since records were first kept.

That is very different from human athletes, who have made constant and dramatic improvements. In an event like the Men's One Mile, for instance, we are now looking at 3 min 45 sec for the world record as compared with 4 min 15 sec in 1910.

Horses, on the other hand, have not been going faster at anything like the same rate; in fact the present record for the Grand National was set in 1973 and for the Cheltenham Gold Cup in 1951. In the Derby, before Kahyasi's electronically timed run in 1988 of 2 min 33.84 sec, the fastest was by Mahmoud in 1936 (2 min 33.8 sec, hand-timed).

This cannot be because horseracing, unlike athletics, has failed to adopt a scientific approach to the subject. Both sports are now far more clued up about health, diet and training methods than they used to be. The main difference is that you can reason with an athlete, but not with a horse.

You can't say to a horse, 'Look, I'm going to start a training programme with you tomorrow. For the next three months I'm going to work you hard, morning and evening. You can have a day off each week, but you have got to be prepared to work really hard because in three months' time you are going to be running for your life. And if you're no bloody good, we're going to get rid of you.'

Horses are not open to that kind of approach. Horses don't like a lot of training. It's all right for a 10-stone man to clock up 70 miles a week in training, but a half-ton racehorse gets very upset if you ask it to gallop more than about nine miles a week. You try taking a horse out in the morning, and then again in the afternoon; at the end of a week you won't have a racehorse left. Every time it sees you coming across the yard with the saddle and bridle in your hand, the horse will break into a sweat; its eyes begin to pop out, it goes off its food straight away. You've had it.

Loads of people have tried to build up a horse's speed and stamina with human-type training methods, but they never get anywhere. Circuit training for instance. They start with the idea of getting the horse to canter up for five furlongs, then walk back, canter up again and walk back. The horse goes off its head; it doesn't understand what it's being asked to do. You can't explain it, like you could to an athlete, and after a couple of these circuits the horse is buzzing, confused. It won't relax and walk, because it's waiting for the next canter, so it jig-jogs along until it's asked to run on again. Beyond a certain, fairly basic point, organized training is beyond a horse's comprehension.

BEWARE THE INTELLIGENT HORSE

People have experimented with all kinds of food additives and wonder-diets to make horses go faster, and for proof of that you only have to look at the number of substances which are now officially proscribed. Mars Bars, for example, are not allowed; they may be all right for humans but racing people are barred from giving them to horses because of the caffeine content. This is enough to show up in a dope-test, so trainers have to be very careful. The same applies to certain ointments and creams which may be effective in treating a particular injury but they can't be used because of some chemical in their content which is on the proscribed list.

A serious amount of money is invested each year in research aimed at inducing horses to run faster. Ultimately, it comes back to the old truth that the greatest ambition of owners, trainers and jockeys is to have winners. First is first, second is nowhere.

Personally, I think you can overdo the artificial, scientific methods. It is hard enough to get Nature, in the form of a racehorse, on your side and working for you. Perhaps that is why I favour the willing, friendly, none-too-bright horse who doesn't need much persuading to get in there and do battle, and run his heart out for you if that is what needs to be done. Such horses are refreshingly unlike the so-called intelligent horses who spend too much time thinking about work instead of doing it, and usually reach the conclusion that racing is not worth the effort.

I had a horse once who was a good prospect, so I put him into a race. He was doing all right until just after the second fence, when something disturbed him and he pulled up. He wasn't lame, so the jockey walked him back. We could find nothing wrong with the horse and eventually he went home in his box. For the rest of his brief racing career that horse never went more than a few yards past the second fence. Then he pulled up. I am not saying he was intelligent, but he had definitely sussed out that there was an easier way to live than running the full distance.

Talking of speed, a cunning old trainer was at Sandown one day. He was standing with the owner and they'd just finished saddling up when the trainer slipped the horse a sugar lump. A steward saw it happen, and came running over.

'I've just seen what you did,' called the steward in that pointed way they speak when they think they're on to something.

'What do you mean?' said the trainer.

'I saw you give that horse a sugar lump.'

The trainer pulled a face. 'Look,' he said, 'it's perfectly all right. There's no funny stuff here. I'll show you.' He took two more lumps out of his pocket, ate one and gave the other to the owner who followed suit. This really embarrassed the steward who began to apologize, saying they'd had a lot of trouble recently with people doping their horses, etc., etc.

'That's all right,' said the trainer, and they went into the paddock. Lester Piggott was riding the horse that day, and he came over to receive his instructions.

'We've been stopping this horse for about a year and a half,' said the trainer to Lester, 'and today's the day we're having the money on him. I want you to bounce him out of the stalls, sit in fifth or sixth for the first four furlongs, then move him up gradually. Have him about second with two furlongs to go, then take up the running a furlong from home. Oh, and don't worry if anything comes past you – it will be either me or the owner!'

BUT WILL IT JUMP?

With Every New Horse, The Last Thing The Jockey Discovers Is Whether It Can Jump

When you ride hundreds of horses in a season, there isn't a lot of time to get attached to a particular animal. With most, I used to get on it in the paddock, sit on it, ride it for maybe five minutes, and get off again. End of relationship, at least until the next time and quite often there wasn't a next time.

If you ride out at home on a horse, obviously you will know it that much better, and if you get a really good horse to ride you would be a strange jockey if you didn't feel admiration for it. But it is only very infrequently, with the rare or exceptional horse, that you develop a special kind of feeling for it. This can be for all sorts of different reasons. One horse I had a soft spot for was Sea Image. He was a marvellous trier; not the most natural jumper in the world, not the fastest or the prettiest horse I have ever ridden, but he would never give up. If there was another horse in front of him, Sea Image would try his hardest to get past and win the race. He didn't always succeed, but then I didn't always expect him to.

As a group, the horses I liked most were the best jumpers – and there was more than one good reason for that. Suppose you are getting on a horse in the paddock and this is the first time you have seen it. Very soon, well before you get down to the start, you can tell what sort of a horse you are riding. You won't know its every characteristic, of course, but it will have fallen into one of the categories into which you with your experience of *x* hundred races have learned to divide horses. It is a smooth mover, for instance; it has a nice mouth and pulls up when you want it to; it turns, and seems to have a good awareness of what is going on around it.

Fine, in that case it looks as though you are in for a nice ride. So long as it can jump! It is one of the mysteries of jump-racing that the horse's ability in the air is the last thing the jockey finds out about, and then only once the race has started.

Well, perhaps not always. When this happened to me, and I felt uneasy about the horse, usually it was because I didn't know the people I was riding for particularly well. Were they giving me an honest account of it or just telling me some story they thought I would like to hear? It is not always easy to tell. Then there was the horse itself. Perhaps it was a flat racer which had only recently turned to hurdles and had no real jumping history.

Faced with such an animal, I would feel a strong urge to do something illegal and pop it over the first hurdle going down to the start – just to make sure that it knew its job and also to put my mind at rest.

I remember doing this one day along with another jockey. We were about last going down to the start and I said to this lad, 'Come on, I don't like the feel this one is giving me. Let's jump the first hurdle on them, down the far side where we won't be seen.'

A few minutes earlier, another jockey in the same race had fallen off his horse as he was leaving the paddock. After shedding his rider, the horse had carried on and followed the other runners down to the start. Seeing this, the jockey had picked himself up and run across the middle of the course to try and catch up with his ride and remount it in time for the race.

For some reason I had not noticed any of this. The two of us turned and jumped the hurdle. As we did so, the jockey with no horse reached our side of the racecourse. Unseen by us, he put his head under the railing and ran along behind our hurdle. Over the top we came – crash! and bowled him over. There was a Stewards' Inquiry about that.

No good me using this as an excuse when I appeared before the stewards, but in France they don't actually mind you jumping a hurdle before the race. It's common practice, on the way down to the start, to pause for a moment and turn and jump a hurdle. In theory it settles the horse down and shows the jockey what it can do.

Peter Scudamore went over to France once and his horse fell at the practice hurdle. It didn't fill him with confidence about his prospects in the race.

Occasionally you get a horse which falls while schooling at home. It doesn't happen often but it's still not a very good sign. One morning I schooled a horse called Credibility. It was a cold morning – and very foggy. The horse was due to run in the Hennessy Gold Cup in a few days' time. We put blinkers on him to make him less nervous in the foggy conditions, and off we went.

As we came to the first fence, the horse reached his take-off stride just at the moment his instinct told him he didn't want to jump. He was going too fast to stop, and instead of leaping upwards he hardly took off at all and just sailed forward at the fence. Half of him got through and half did not. He ended up straddled across the fence, hopelessly stuck with all his legs off the ground.

I had a much better landing. I just stepped off him onto the top rail of the fence and jumped down, unhurt. It took three of us to pull the horse off the fence, and he must have had a sore belly for several days. Credibility. What an unfortunate name that was.

NOW GET OUT OF THIS

Improvisation – That's The Name Of The Game When All Else Fails

You are in second place, tracking the leading horse. The trainer has already said, 'Whatever you do, don't hit the front before the last two furlongs.' If he is right about this, it means you are riding one of those horses which, if it doesn't actually stop, won't try nearly as hard when it is in the lead and can't see another horse in front of it.

You come up to the next fence, still half a mile from home, and the horse in front falls. You jump the fence all right, but now you are in the lead. Your race plan has suddenly gone crazy – and so has the trainer but luckily you can't see him. What do you do next?

The short answer is nothing. You are sunk. There is nothing at all you can do about it except hope and pray that your horse keeps on galloping until it has crossed the line.

In that situation there is no hope of improvising your way out of trouble, but there are many other times when you can still help yourself. Fred Winter was riding a horse called Mandarin in the French Grand National when the horse's bit broke. It was after he'd jumped about the third fence, and on a very big track he had an awful long way to go without any reins. Somehow, he kept himself on the horse and the other jockeys helped to keep him in on the bends so he didn't go shooting off out of the race. Quite how he steered the horse I don't know; it must have been some private combination of technique and determination which carried him through – and he won the race.

That was before my time, of course, although I have seen pictures of it. Another out-of-the-way incident I can remember was at Deauville when Lester Piggott lost his stick in a race with about a furlong and a half to go. Lester wasn't going to take that sitting down, so he moved alongside a horse ridden by Alain Lequeux, got into the other jockey's rhythm, then leaned over and snatched his stick out of his hand. Lester finished the race using the other feller's whip. The crowd loved it, but Lester's reward was a fine.

NOW GET OUT OF THIS

At Plumpton one day I was racing down the hill when a horse turned over in front of me. It was ridden by Chris Reed, and for some reason his stick went miles in the air and when it came down I caught it, rode on and finished the race carrying two sticks.

Now that everything is filmed in such detail – from patrol vans running alongside the course and other cameras filming from front-on as the horses come up to the winning post – there isn't much room for practical jokes. If you do it on the far side and before you get to the straight, you may be able to reach over and pull another jockey's foot out of his iron – which causes him to hang on a bit tight for a while – but nowadays you don't get a lot of messing about. Real life throws up enough ridiculous moments to keep the average jockey quiet – and what is amazing is how everybody copes so well when the moment comes.

Thinking of jockeys losing their irons, I have seen this happen on several occasions. The stirrup iron breaks, but the jockey still keeps control of the horse, and even wins the race. A couple of weeks ago at Chepstow, a horse fell at the last fence, got back on its feet, the jockey remounted it and they were so far in front of the other runners that they still came in first.

In the closing stages of a race, when the leading horses are giving their all, the whips are out and there is always that temptation for the jockey to give his horse one more whack. I am not talking here about lazy horses who need keeping up to their work, but about normal good horses who want to run and try and do their best for whoever is riding them.

I don't like to see all this whacking because I don't think it is necessary. My old Governor, Fred Winter, said, 'If it won't go for three it won't go for twenty-three,' and I agree with that. But it is a very difficult area to legislate for and the debate goes on and on. So much depends on the view of the individual. I rode a couple of races on a horse called Observe: one day I was fined for being too hard on him, and the next time I rode him I was fined for being too easy on him.

It has been suggested that a limit could be imposed, so that a jockey would be allowed to hit the horse six times, say, and no more. This would mean a lot of jockeys would have to go to night school and be taught to count that far, but, seriously, I am not sure that you can make rules which are good for all horses. As I see it, the vast majority of horses are bred for racing and all they want to do is go forward as fast as they can. They want to do their best, and hitting them with a stick won't make them go any faster.

In some places, Scandinavia for instance, sticks are banned, and the only reason I would advocate carrying a stick at all is to keep the horse going in a straight line. If you have a horse that tries to run out with you, it is very handy to have a stick and give it a crack down the shoulder.

Bolters are another matter. With them you just have to try

everything you can think of to stay on the horse and get it calmed down.

My best friend when I was an apprentice was a lad called Victor Soane. We went off one day after work to school for Godfrey Burr, for whom, incidentally, I rode my first winner. Victor and I were riding two fillies which, to complicate matters, were not only scatty but twins as well.

When we had finished schooling them, we set off back for the stables. It was just getting dark and Victor's horse was particularly frisky, fly-jumping every few paces and trying to run off with him. Our route took us down a long concrete road to the farmyard. Victor's horse would not give up, she kept on jumping and jigging about, and perhaps Victor was feeling a little bit tired at the end of a fairly long day. At any rate, the filly suddenly gave one jerk which seemed to catch him by surprise – and she was off.

By then it was almost completely dark and all I could see, as I looked down the concrete road, was Victor's white helmet tearing away from me at about a thousand miles an hour. I knew there was a sharp bend he had to get round before the farmyard, and as he vanished into the blackness I was sure he was going to be thrown off.

I know you shouldn't laugh at other people's misfortune – even when it's your best friend, or especially because it's your best friend – but when things like that happen, laughing is about all you can do.

What happened to Victor? Oh, well, if you really want to know he fought the horse, got it back under control and pulled it up just before they reached the farmyard. There's nothing to it, really – when you have a happy ending.

AGAINST THE ODDS

Not Many Punters Really Expect To Win, But Racing Could Do More To Help Them Enjoy Their Sport

As I write, they are just starting a new clampdown. They think that one or two jockeys have been betting, so they have to be seen to be doing something about it. This time the word is that they are going to tighten the rules so hard, the problem will be throttled once and for all. I wish them luck, but I think they are naive if they expect to succeed any more than they have done in the past.

It's an impossible situation. The ground rules might seem to be clear. A jockey must not bet on horse races, nor can he be associated with someone who does bet. That includes giving people tips. So far so good. Or is it? Obviously there must be some forms of control. A jockey can't go out and stop a horse from winning and think he is going to get away with it. In next to no time the whole sport would be undermined.

That much is wrong, I agree. But I can't help thinking that it wouldn't bring about the end of civilization as we know it to allow jockeys to place a simple bet if they wanted to. If this could be allowed, it would get rid of a lot of awkward situations which under existing rules and attitudes are very difficult to adjudge fairly.

A jockey opens the door to the postman. That day he has got three rides and the postman knows all about this. He is a keen betting man and he has looked up the runners in his newspaper.

'Morning,' he says to the jockey. 'I see you're riding Beachcomber today. Do you fancy it?'

'Yes,' says the jockey, who thinks it has a reasonable chance even if it's not a brilliant horse.

Wrong! Technically, that counts as tipping, and he should not have said anything to the postman which might influence any bets he is likely to place.

Even more ridiculous is the scene where a jockey goes on television before a race.

'What do you think your chances are?' the interviewer asks him.

'Well, he should run very well,' says the jockey. 'I've been quite impressed with him all year and just lately he's been doing very well in training . . .'

Wrong again! That is tipping too, although, admittedly, the jockey would be very unlucky if he was had up for it. Once you are on television, you have got to say something, and it would be a brave or foolish man who said, 'He's useless, got no chance.' As jockeys well know, owners don't much like to hear that sort of thing.

You could, of course, go to the heart of the problem and abolish bookmakers altogether. Unfortunately, that wouldn't be so clever because without bookmakers there would be no racing. In this country racing is run by the bookmakers, and it's no good anyone kidding themselves that it isn't. True, the bookmakers also put a lot into the sport, but they take an awful lot out as well.

An ideal solution, to my mind, would be to set up a Tote monopoly, with bookmakers allowed on-course only. There is no doubt that bookmakers add a great deal to the atmosphere of a day's racing. You get thirty of them stood in a line calling the odds, with all the paraphernalia of their special stand, the satchel for the money, the bloke who writes the bets in a register, the tic-tac men and the chalky dramatics each time they change the odds on the board. The racing public like to see the bookies, and to do business with them, even though most punters realize that the odds are stacked against them. The bookie nearly always wins, but the punter at the course doesn't seem to mind this. It's all part of the entertainment.

In Australia they have a system whereby the betting shops are owned by the Government, and so more of the revenue, after paying out the winners and deducting expenses, goes back into racing. At present in Britain the owners of the betting shops negotiate through their association, BOLA, how much of their profits must be returned to racing. Not surprisingly, the people who negotiate on behalf of BOLA (it stands for Betting Office

Licensees Association) are very switched on and are able to secure a good bargain – which of course means that less money is available to finance the sport than would be available if the State controlled the betting shops.

At least, though, our Government has recently tried to increase the proportion of on-course betting by making winnings tax-free if the bet is made at the course. Bets made in a betting shop are taxable, and for regular punters this amounts to a big incentive to get up and go to the races.

Against that is a new system called Satellite Information

Services (SIS) which has already been installed in quite a few betting shops. This virtually guarantees an on-tap supply of televised racing. Today, for instance, as I write this, there is no racing on the four television channels but if I went into the right betting shop I could watch, via satellite, racing coverage from Folkestone and Ludlow. This, of course, is a big incentive for people not to go racing. No journey to the races, no admission, no being charged exorbitant prices for food and drinks – all you have to do is go to the betting shop and see it there.

I think this satellite system is going to make a big difference to bookmakers' profits and also to the number of people who go racing. It will be interesting to see how it turns out, but on the face of it I reckon the bookmakers – who have a 40% stake in SIS, with the rest being floated off into private ownership – have made a good move for themselves. In future, when racing is cancelled in Britain, as it often is in the winter, SIS will be able to beam in live coverage from the Continent, from Sweden, Germany, France and other places so that the punter will nearly always have something to bet on.

Quite where that is going to leave racing in Britain, remains to be seen. I certainly think that the sport itself has missed an opportunity by not taking a sizeable interest in the venture. The income from the profits is something that could have been put to very good use in the coming years to ensure that racecourse facilities are kept up to date and competitive with all the other schemes and entertainments offered by rival branches of the sports and leisure industry.

In April this year I started a club which now has more than 3,000 members. It's called the Racing and Punters Club and its main function is to work as a tipping service. We aim to be more selective and to give punters more information than they get through the press and television. Since we began, we are £3000 up for a £10 level stake, which is good going. As with all betting, it is the bookmaker who wins eventually but at the moment we are having a good run. Our members seem to like the service we give them; they aren't daft enough to think they will always win, and meanwhile they are happy in the knowledge that they are now making better, more informed bets than they used to and so they are in with a better long-term chance of not losing too much.

From the beginning we tried to increase the punters' interest by leasing our own horses. I still think this is a good idea, since anyone with even a modest stake in a racehorse is going to feel more involved and get more out of the sport. Unfortunately, it hasn't gone as well as we hoped because the first six horses we got all broke down before they even reached a racecourse. Now we have just got another one and I am very much hoping that he stays fit longer than the others, but you never know.

We also run a number of club outings. We took sixty people over to the Arc de Triomphe recently and we reckon to take a tent at the big meetings in England like Cheltenham and Ascot. Members can come and spend the day with us, watch the racing on closed-circuit television and have a bet – all without going outside if they don't want to. It all helps to make the day-out more enjoyable. We hold dinner-dances as well, and we keep the membership fee low so that people are getting good value.

I think that this is a direction that a lot of people will want to follow in the future. It is time the format of a 'day at the races' was looked at seriously and changed to make it more attractive, especially to younger people. Racing needs more younger people under the age of thirty – its next generation of regular spectators – and it won't get them by leaving things as they are.

The kind of innovations I have in mind include putting on live entertainment before and even during the meeting – difficult in our winters, I know, but not impossible in the summer – and having a mobile casino on the course. A big percentage of the people who come through the gates every day are there to bet. They aren't all that interested in going along to the paddock each time, and for them the twenty-five minute wait between races is a long time. If other betting attractions were laid on for them, I am convinced they would be popular and well used.

At Cheltenham they have stalls selling country clothes, sporting prints, leather goods, saddlery, jewellery and various other things. They do a very good trade because they appeal, especially, to women who may not be all that keen on the racing. They have come along with husbands who enjoy following the horses and betting, and they are happy to wander off round the stalls and see if there is something they fancy. Cheltenham is, admittedly, a very well-supported meeting, so the stallholders know it will be worth their while turning up.

Wolverhampton on a Monday afternoon would be a different proposition. With the crowds they get at Wolverhampton, it would be difficult to sell an umbrella in the pouring rain. However, you have to start somewhere if you are going to make an impression on the market, and I am quite certain there are a lot of middle-range courses which would do nicely if they managed the business side of their operation with a more adventurous spirit.

DUELLING WITH MONEY

At The Sales – The Agony And The Ecstasy

Whether you go as a seller or a buyer, a day at the Sales is like a long walk through a minefield. I was at Doncaster the other day. It's no worse than other Horse Sales, but you certainly don't go there to enjoy yourself.

Every year there seem to be more and more horses on the market which have something wrong with them. For the seller it is now relatively easy to patch up a horse with a bad leg so it will get through the Sales. Only when the buyer gets it home, and it goes lame the next day, is the truth revealed. The effect of an earlier spell of bandaging has worn off, but the leg is still weak; or the effect of some drug or other has worn off and the leg begins to swell up. What you thought was a really nice horse is just another case for treatment, and it may be a long time before you can put it to any kind of real test.

The buyer does have some forms of redress if he has bought a bad 'un. If the horse is a 'crib-biter', for instance, and starts biting the top of the stable door or grabbing on to things with its teeth, that is one of a small number of classified vices. The buyer then has the right to send back the horse within 48 hours, or some other agreed time limit, and the sale is void. He needs a vet's certificate as well, and not all Sales make allowance for this, but it is fairly widely recognized now. Another vice is if the horse is a 'windsucker', and sucks in a lot of air, or it has been tubed or operated on for unsoundness in wind and the seller has not disclosed this when he put the horse into the Sale. The same rule may also apply to 'whistlers' and 'roarers', which indicate certain types of breathing problem.

However, if you get a horse home from the Sale and it goes lame the next day, there is nothing more you can do about it except pray to God that it suddenly develops a taste for chewing lumps off the stable door. Otherwise, you are stuck with it. If you bought it for someone else, you can still hope to sell it on. Alternatively, you may decide to put it straight back into the Sale, but you can be sure that when it goes round again you will lose quite a lot of money on it. The only other option is to patch up the horse, put it out in a field for a year and see what happens. That's expensive too. It's a nightmare.

Horse Sales are big business. This one at Doncaster lasted for five full days and the huge catalogue, with all the horses' pedigrees and other details, makes a nice doorstop when you bring it home. There is one sale ring, about thirty feet in diameter, where the auctioneer does his work faced by all the prospective buyers who position themselves on rows of banked-up seating where they can get a good view of the horses being led in. Round and about are several hundred stables allocated to the horses in the Sale, and places where likely bidders wanting a preview can see the animals walk up and down and show off their paces.

The people who gather at the ring are a very mixed bunch indeed. Trainers, owners and breeders make up a large part of the crowd. Near the entrance where the horses are led in you will see a small bunch of dealers. In the course of a Sale they may buy ten or a dozen horses each, not always with a particular owner in mind but just to add to the stock of horses from which they make their living. A lot of people buy regularly from dealers whose judgment they trust; if they buy one on spec and it turns out well, they reckon the dealer is a sound bloke who knows what he is looking for and they go back to him the next time they want a horse.

You find showjumping and eventing people there as well. Mostly they turn up just in case there is a horse which takes their fancy. You also get a few tourists who like to watch the horses going through, and some posers who sit there all day with their catalogues open and never buy a single horse between them. Heaven knows why they come; they seem to think it's the thing to do.

This motley band now waits for its leader, the man who will orchestrate the whole show and by his professional skills extract mountainous sums (he hopes) of guineas (it's still always done in guineas) from the wallets of the buyers and transfer them, less commission, to the wallets of the sellers.

The auctioneer is the man who makes the entire thing go. He is like a banker, a master of ceremonies and a psychologist rolled into one, always pushing, pushing to raise the price higher. Even when a bidder thinks he has reached his limit, the auctioneer who knows his job will still get a couple more bids out of him.

At Newmarket they have a Mr Pimms who certainly knows his job. To say he has the gift of the gab does no justice at all to his range of arguments and quickness of thought. They say it takes two and a half to three minutes to sell a horse at auction, and Mr Pimms understands this better than anyone.

'Come on, come on,' he urges his bidders when they seem to be flagging. 'You've come this far, now here's a lovely horse, you've gone to fifty thousand guineas, now go on, have one more, don't let that feller over there beat you . . .'

Sure enough, he gets it up to fifty-five thousand, then sixty. 'Come on, come on, get your hand in your pocket, this one could be a Derby winner . . .'

And so it goes on. Paying a few thousand guineas extra seems like the most natural thing in the world. Everyone loves a Derby winner, don't they?

To help him, the auctioneer has a team of spotters. They stand in front of the bidders and do nothing but look into the crowd and spot any bidders the auctioneer may have missed; then they point them out to him and the bidding goes on.

Bidding at a Sale is a fascinating business, like duelling with money. If you ever get tempted into it, make sure you've got enough money to cover your last bid. Every so often someone gets this wrong, and when they do they find they have made a very expensive mistake. At the end of an auction the top bidder signs a chit, but if he can't afford to pay for the horse it has to be resubmitted and go through the auction process again. The second time round it is almost certain to go for less, and the bloke who was responsible has to make up the difference between the two prices. Recently this cost someone £30,000, which is silly really. I mean, you can buy a horse for that.

LUCK

Good Luck Is Something That Helps You To Win Races. Bad Luck Is Far Worse

You can make a lot of your own luck, but when things aren't running your way it often seems that this time you're going all the way to the bottom. I can give you a thousand examples, and here's one of them.

Recently, I sent a horse to Cheltenham. I could not see it being beaten. In the race, a furlong from home, my horse was lying second. The horse that was leading then deviated suddenly from the straight line it had been running and brought my horse to a standstill. For a second it went down on one leg, then it recovered and stood up again. In the time this took to happen another horse came up and went past it, so now my horse was third. They finished in that order, and after the race the first horse was disqualified for impeding my animal. But still we didn't win the race because the horse that went past mine had finished second and was declared the winner. It's the way it goes, you tell yourself on the way home.

To take another example – one that often happens in flat racing – you have a horse which is dying to win a race. It's fit and in good form and seems to have everything going for it. Then suddenly, during the race it gets boxed in by a chance combination of things done by other horses. The horse in front tires, but doesn't roll away from the rails and leave a gap, as they do if your luck is in. Meanwhile, the way through on the outside is blocked by a line of unimpeded horses which go streaming past like cars in the fast lane of a motorway – and now your horse is seventh or eighth with no chance of making up the ground. Yes, well, you say to yourself on the way home, if he hadn't got boxed in he could have won that.

Another day, you decide to send a horse to the races because the weather has been good and you know it likes firm going. Then it rains all night long and when you wake up on the morning of the race it takes about two seconds to realize that the rest of the day is going to be a complete waste of time.

IN
WINNERS
ENCLOSURE
COF!
COF!

Luck plays a big part in how a new horse turns out. You buy it at the Sales as a yearling and you keep it all winter, then next year you start working it as a two-year-old. If you are unlucky, it gets a cough and you can't work it properly, and it falls behind the other two-year-olds in the stable. You've already told the owner how good you think it is, so now he gets double-frustrated because he has been dreaming of standing around patting it in the winner's enclosure in front of his mates. Instead of which he is ringing up every day to ask about a sick horse which is making minus progress compared with the competition.

If you are a shade luckier, neither this horse nor any of the others gets a cough and training goes ahead as planned. Fine, but after a while you begin to wonder just how good these two-year-olds are. Up at the gallops they all keep finishing together in a line and you can't be sure if they are all very good or all bloody moderate. You should have more faith, you tell yourself. You thought the horse was good when you bought it and it hasn't let you down yet. All right, we'll run it. A decision is made. You tell the owner and he is delighted.

The day of the race approaches and you are preparing the horse nicely when suddenly it develops sore shins. In this condition, with millions of tiny fractures on the shin-bone or cannon-bone, it obviously can't race and has to be withdrawn. The quickest remedy for sore shins is to send it swimming; this is something that most horses love doing and is very effective. Even so, whether or not you manage to fix it up with some swimming lessons, time has been lost while the horse recovers. When it is better, you have to get it going again. It develops another minor ailment, maybe the cough you thought you had been spared. You rest the horse, get it going again . . . but now the ground is too hard for it. The months have gone by and it's nearly June. You don't want to risk another round of sore shins, do you. 'Can't run it, I'm afraid,' you tell the owner. 'Ground's too firm.'

You don't want to send the horse to race, but you keep it going on the all-weather gallop at home, in the hope that the weather will turn and there will be a little bit of rain. There is rain, but not a little bit; it belts down for two and a half weeks. 'Can't run it,

I'm afraid,' you tell the owner. 'Ground's too soft.' Privately you begin to think that this is an unlucky horse and it will be a miracle if you get it on the racecourse at all that year.

One of two things may then happen. You do get it on the racecourse, and . . . it's useless. Out there at last, after all those months of preparation, the horse puts on a blinding demonstration that it has learnt nothing since you bought it. It beats two others in the race, but that is no consolation at all.

The feelings of despair that now want to consume you would have been even worse, by the way, if this had happened earlier in the year. Then, you've entered your best two-year-old ahead of all the others in the stable, and it performs like the one I have just described. Blimey, you think, if that was my best two-year-old, what am I going to be telling the other owners for the rest of the season?

And yet, the day after the race you have second thoughts. You begin to wonder if this début disaster was all the horse's fault. It did, after all, do well in training and it is still a good-looking horse and moves well. Maybe the distance was wrong, maybe it needs a little bit further. Would it mature more as a three-year-old? Soon enough, a decision is needed: should you keep it all the way through another winter and run it again next year, or should you cut your losses and get rid of it.

All the evidence is carefully weighed, the horse is examined each day for a week, and then you decide. You decide that the answer is no. You should cut your losses and sell the horse. This, with some sadness, you do. Next year it comes out for someone else and never stops winning.

But that's all looking on the dark side of luck. There is, in case anyone has forgotten this, a bright side as well. You have a promising two-year-old who's been working well. Everything goes right for it. It's tough, it doesn't get sore shins, you prepare it for racing and off it goes. From where you are standing at the course you can see your horse from the start. It bolts out of the stalls and comes home an easy winner. And you've backed it.

That's the good side, when all the luck is running for you. The owner goes home delighted and you can't wait to run the horse again. Also, you've got some other horses in the stable which you reckon are just as good, if not better. The future, for the time being, is a nice little bed of roses.

If your luck is in, and holding, you can get away with the most extraordinary things. I rode a horse once for Fred Winter. On the Saturday it pricked its foot while exercising. On Sunday and Monday it was kept in all day to rest. On Tuesday and Wednesday it couldn't go out because of snow. It was led out on Thursday and went for a trot round the roads on Friday. On Friday night the blacksmith was shoeing it. The lad who looked after the horse assumed that the blacksmith would take its head collar off and let it down for the night. The blacksmith,meanwhile, assumed that the lad would do it. As a result, they never mentioned it to each other, so the horse stayed tied up all night. It didn't have any supper because it couldn't reach it, just had to stand there for a whole miserable night.

Next day it went to the races, and won by twenty lengths. Explain the logic in that.

SEX

The Obsession Of Horse People. Why?

I can't account for it, but if there is one subject of conversation which consumes the thoughts of the people I work with, it is sex. It doesn't matter what company you are in, the talk is always the same. And sometimes the action.

I have written elsewhere of the rocking hostel beds on a Sunday evening, when I had just started as a young apprentice and some of the other lads were entertaining their girlfriends in the urgent style which was so typical of their mating habits. If it had been simply a question of waiting until they could get a bit of privacy, perhaps they would have waited. But in our hostel, with three small bedrooms shared between twelve apprentices, there was no chance of privacy, however long they waited. The only alternative they could see themselves faced with was going without – and that was totally unacceptable. Besides, they were more pleased than a pack of puppies to be reunited with their girlfriends – and some of these ladies had travelled from places as far away as Swindon and Wantage to be with them on their afternoon off. So, two by two, into the bunks they went, and never mind a few squeaky springs.

Perhaps it has to do with the outdoor life. Jockeys and stable lads are probably fitter and more full of life than most of the working population, and so they have more energy to spare at the end of their day. In the weighing room it is, if anything, worse, though this is not entirely unexpected. You put forty blokes into a room together, and one of them is bound to want to tell the others about something naughty he was getting up to the night before. And don't you tell me there aren't thirty-nine pairs of ears only too happy to listen to his story.

When women jockeys first arrived in National Hunt racing, some of us weren't too sure how they would settle down. None of the lads wanted to tone down their language, but from the beginning that was never a problem. Some of the girls can give back just as good as anything thrown at them and, in any case, they didn't change with us but had their own weighing room. At

first this was usually a caravan with fairly limited facilities, but nowadays they have their own proper weighing room and live their own lives in there. Don't ask me what they talk about

because I have never tried to listen in – but I will tell you that one or two of them are quite keen on invading the boys' changing room before the lads have finished in the showers. However, the lads look upon that as high spirits and try not to take much notice.

Where you do notice a difference is in Italy. I used to go over to race in Milan and Rome, and there the women jockeys change in the same weighing room as the fellers. When I first went, and found these women stripping off in the same room, I couldn't believe it. I suppose they reckon it's no worse than changing on the beach, so they just get on with it. I couldn't understand everything that was being said, mind you, but the Italian fellers didn't seem to object to having a bit of female company.

In Britain, the subject of sex is not limited to stable lads and jockeys. All horse people are the same. Showjumpers, three-day eventers, the hunting crowd – they are all at it, and not just in the mind. If you are following a hunt, take your eyes away from the leaders galloping away after the dogs and you will notice all kinds of things – couples filtering off into the woods or sneaking back to the horsebox for a quiet half-hour together. There must be something about all that fresh air, especially in winter, which inspires horsemen and horsewomen to do things in seconds which it would take them months to get round to indoors.

And the clothes. Let's not forget the clothes. Some women do undoubtedly look very attractive when they wear jodhpurs, black boots and a smart, well-cut hunting jacket. It's the lure of the uniform, I suppose. A lot of men go for that kind of thing. I can see it does have romantic possibilities, even if it is not a particular fixation with me. As for what is, I am not saying. It's a retired jockey's privilege to take his secrets with him.

MANURE

The Stuff That Makes Your Garden Grow

The only reason I became interested in horse-racing was that my dad, who was a fireman on the railway, won a race horse in a raffle. The prize was limited to the horse itself; no feed, training fees or anything like that. So my father, who was earning about twenty quid a week in those days, had to see what he could fix up for the horse.

First of all he rang Fulke Walwyn to see how much he would charge for training fees. Fulke quoted him fifty-five pounds a week plus all the extras for blacksmith, vet and so on. Dad said, 'It's very kind of you, but that's too expensive for me. I'll have to try somewhere else.'

So then he rang Neville Crump, in the North, but Neville was almost as expensive as Fulke Walwyn. Dad wondered who to try next, and he thought of Fred Winter. It was a lucky thought because Fred was just getting started at the time, and when my father 'phoned him he said he'd train the horse for five pounds a week. Dad was delighted. Not only was the price a lot lower than the others, but Fred lived close by as well, so we could all go over and see the horse as much as we wanted.

'That seems fine,' said Dad. 'I'd like you to take him on. There's just one other thing, though. My wife and I are very keen gardeners, so will it be all right if we come over at the weekends and pick up some manure for the garden?'

Fred said, 'For five pounds a week there won't be any manure.'

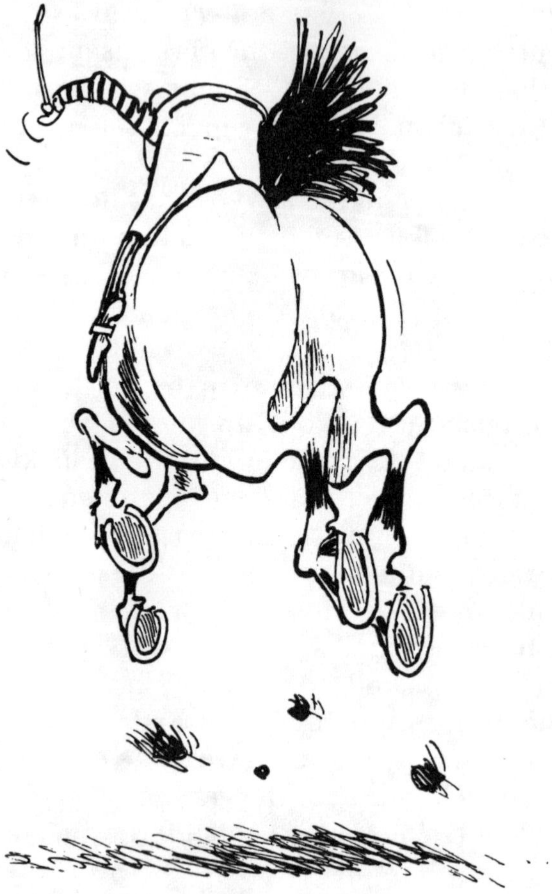